# CLAIMED BY GOD
# FOR MISSION

# CLAIMED BY GOD FOR MISSION

## The Congregation Seeks New Forms

## Eugene L. Stockwell

WORLD OUTLOOK PRESS • 475 Riverside Drive • New York, New York

All Biblical quotations are taken from *The New
English Bible: New Testament.* © The Delegates of
the Oxford University Press and The Syndics of The
Cambridge University Press 1961.
*Reprinted by permission.*

LIBRARY OF CONGRESS CATALOG NUMBER 65-26749

FIRST EDITION

*book design by* JOHN R. HUDSON, JR.
PRINTED AND BOUND BY THE PARTHENON PRESS, NASHVILLE, TENNESSEE
SB5-MPH-6-65-40M

# contents

TO PEG

and

BILL, BOB, MARTHY, DICKY

# foreword

WE LIVE in an ecumenical age. We welcome the increasing recognition that in one world the Christian gospel must be one witness.

We aso live in a differentiated world. Split up in nations and ideologies, functions and denominations, we welcome every variety of faithful response to the Christian gospel.

To be the church in this ecumenical and differentiated world is fascinatingly difficult. To combine the simplicity and openness of early childhood with the incisive analysis and ambiguity of adulthood calls for resources no human being has of himself. To seek to know the way, even the next step on the way, forces us into a dependence upon resources only God can make available.

By his creation and preservation of us all, God holds a claim upon us, upon the whole wide world. He also holds a claim upon the church. We here set out to explore some aspects of the nature of this claim. Our special concern is the missionary structure of the local congregation.

This inquiry is open to any approach we choose to take. The agenda of the congregation in this ecumenical and differentiated age, however, is not ours to determine at will: it is to a large degree set for us by God's Word and God's world. We shall attempt to seek out implications of this agenda for developing forms of our congregational life.

Why a special study book for Methodists on this topic? First, to share within our Methodist communion some of the issues and ideas raised up by fellow Christians across the world in the wide-ranging ecumenical discussion afoot today on the congregational structures most appropriate to a renewed participation in God's mission in history. Second, whatever differentiates us as Methodists from other Christians—a differentiation of secondary importance but nonetheless real—calls for our own serious reflection upon the issues of congregational life and forms in order that our partial contribution to the whole ecumenical discussion may be informed and relevant.

I want to record two recent experiences of very different kinds that have some bearing upon this study book.

One was a weekend spent at the Ecumenical Institute in Chicago, organized and functioning under the inspiration and aegis of Joseph Mathews. Whatever one may think about the work and service of this Institute—its very manner of operation encourages discussion and highly contrasting opinions—here is a group of families living as a disciplined Christian community avowedly out to shake up the comfortable church patterns of our day. They are determined, to use their language, "to participate radically in the contemporary civilizing process." I went there to participate in a weekend study on the local congregation. What I encountered was, again to use their terms, a weekend of "Christian brainwashing" of the most intensive sort which helped me to gain some new insights into ways in which a congregation can get hold of some handles that may help it in its participation in God's mission in our world. At a number of points in this study book there will appear, often unheralded, some concepts that for me came out of that fruitful weekend. I was told at the Ecumenical Institute that those living there steal each other's material mercilessly. I am pleased to share in their sport.

The second experience was to read a book at one sitting as I flew from New York to Los Angeles. It is David Wilkerson's *The Cross and the Switchblade*.[1] It had been recommended to a group of us a few days before by Robert Miller, assistant to the President of Union Theological Seminary. It is the story of the author, an

---

[1] Published by Bernard Geis Associates, distributed by Random House, 1963.

8

Assembly of God pastor, who understood God's guidance to mean he should leave his Pennsylvania pastorate to plunge into the heart of New York City and to become passionately involved in assistance to, and relationship with, teen-agers in the grip of loneliness, narcotics, broken homes, and meaninglessness. He deals more with the teen-age problem than he does with church structures that might meet the problem. Most impressive is his simple, profound trust in the Holy Spirit to perform in our day what most of us, and he himself, cannot describe otherwise than as miracles. As I read I could not help but believe that Methodist congregations could profit mightily from some of the unconditional reliance on prayer and the power of God to which David Wilkerson testifies.

A very penetrating analysis of the theme of "the missionary structure of the congregation" written in Asia [2] concludes with a three-page chapter entitled "Words, Words, Words!" and it raises this question in its first sentence: "Why is it that the intensive re-exploration of the Bible in the light of today's completely changed circumstances has yielded such a rich harvest of new and inspiring theological insights, but that notwithstanding this, the churches as a whole appear to be in a very deep rut?" Some may consider it naive, but increasingly I believe that the renewal of church life and structures, so crucial in our day, will demand the hardest and most radical thought of which all churchmen are capable combined with the most simple trust and expectant attitude which really believes God will perform specific miracles in our day and in our presence. If most Christian congregations are to be new and vital, we must pray for a miracle. I doubt that God wishes to give us anything less.

\* \* \* \* \*

It is impossible to encompass in a paragraph my gratitude to many who have helped this manuscript on its way towards completion. Dr.

---

[2] John Fleming and Ken Wright, *Structures for a Missionary Congregation*, East Asia Christian Conference, 1964.

Henry Sprinkle and the study book committee of the Joint Commission on Education and Cultivation of the Methodist Board of Missions have been both sympathetic and prodding. A rather large number of friends and colleagues, laymen and clergy, read early drafts and were most helpful with forthright comment. In particular I owe a debt of appreciation to Dr. Tracey K. Jones, Jr., who in honesty did not hold back frank comment and in kindness phrased it so as to strengthen our daily friendship. My wife and children, to whom this book is dedicated, deserve more than any words can express. With their encouragement, for days I simply checked out of family life to engage in this modest task. Finally, to Mrs. Pat Ewald, my secretary, goes my gratitude for patience and order in sorting out the vagaries of authorship from the administration of a busy office with consummate skill.

EUGENE L. STOCKWELL

## OUT OF THIS WORLD

I HAD A DREAM last night. A wild, improbable kind of dream. The kind of thing that just could not happen, but in the dream it did.

It was about my local church over on Piermont Street. Suddenly everything we had taken for granted as part of the life of our congregation was swept away. Nothing *had* to be what it had always been before.

There was no bishop, no district superintendent, no pastor to run things. There were no appropriations that had to be met, no commitments to any program, nothing that had to be done simply because it had to be done. Everything was wide open. There were no schedules, no fixed meeting times, no standing committees that had to meet. There was no budget, no book of rules, no assured income, no plan of work, no church organization, no Sunday school, no woman's society, no youth fellowship, no men's group, no church bulletin, no sermon in the works. I did not approve of all this, but that was the dream.

It all happened very suddenly. A few of us were sitting around the church lounge, near the fireplace, talking about our new situation. We did not know why this had come about, and apparently we did not care to delve into that.

We knew three things. One was that we felt wonderfully free. Not to have to do all those things we had always thought we had to do in church was unbelievable. We never had realized before what a burden they were to us. Just to sit there and know that nothing had to be accomplished, nothing approved, nothing planned was a great relief.

The second thing we knew was that underneath our sense of freedom, rather mixed up with it, was a certain touch of insecurity. We were glad that we were free, but we were just a bit anxious about the future. If all our old congregational securities were swept away, what was left? We could not quite decide to disband completely, but we had little idea of why we should remain together. It was a bit frightening, exhilarating, disturbing, adventurous, all in one.

The third thing we knew was that this would not last. We had three months—no more—to be and do what as a congregation we wanted to be and do. We could wait out the three months and return to our old patterns, reinstating all the usual plans, programs and schedules; or we could use those three months to start something entirely new which might make the old unnecessary. In three months the bishop, district superintendent, pastor, committees, and programs would all return. Our question was whether these three months would make any difference.

Sitting over near the piano there was a young fellow dressed in a sport coat and slacks. His maroon shirt was open at the collar. He appeared to be entirely relaxed, comfortable, quiet. He had his legs crossed in an irreverent sort of way. His smile was quizzical, friendly, natural. We wondered who he was.

Conversation developed slowly. We were in no rush. No one had to leave. Nothing special had to be said. Inevitably, however, it drifted around to what we would do with the next three months. Would we do nothing? That was tempting and easy but hardly satisfying. We could not agree that these three free months, so unexpectedly ours, would be ignored as though they did not exist. Would we plan a careful program of meetings, services, activities, a bazaar, a church supper, and a financial drive? That was the last thing we would want to do. For three months we had been de-

12

livered from that. But if old structures were gone, we knew that inevitably new ones would soon appear.

Eventually we got around to a central question we discussed at length. It seemed that every topic that came up led us back to this question: What does it mean to be a Christian congregation anyway? Some of us rebelled at the question, but we could not escape it. It came up in many forms. Sometimes it was, Why are we here? Other times it was, What valid reasons keep us together as a congregation? Occasionally it was, What are our real priorities?

We got into some pretty fundamental matters which were not at all clear to us. We sensed that however free we might be temporarily of old patterns, we were certainly not free from a struggle. There was the personal struggle each one of us began to undergo. To raise questions about our congregational life immediately meant we had to raise questions about ourselves as individuals. Who am I? What does it mean to be a person? What are my real priorities? It was an agonizing experience. Three months of this would do us in.

And there was the group struggle. If we were perfectly free as a group to be what we wanted to be, what did we want to be?

The strange young fellow in sport jacket and slacks seemed to be trying to get a word in, but we didn't get what he wanted to say to us.

It took a lot of time to work through all this. Days shaded off into weeks, and weeks became a month, then two months, almost three. Our period of grace was about up. We found no simple answers. We even decided that no such answers existed. Nevertheless, four affirmations did take meaning for us.

The first was that as a congregation we existed not for ourselves but for others. We could not think of one good reason to stay together and live and act as a congregation except as our being together was a preparation for life and service beyond ourselves, in the middle of the world. There just was no sufficient reason to be a

13

congregation unless the life of that congregation was turned outward to all that was going on around it. As a people we had—please forgive the word—a *mission*. We could not spell out the full extent of that mission, but we knew deep down that we could not get away from it and still be a Christian congregation. We also knew that every single plan, scheme, or form of work we might devise for ourselves as a congregation had to be tied to that mission which looked outward, at others, at the wide world around us.

Secondly, we affirmed that we must know how to die. It surprised us how much we talked about death. This came up first when someone casually commented that the disappearance of all the old forms during these three months was like their very death. We began to play with this idea. Death was not so bad, seen in that light. Death was almost welcomed. Not our own personal, physical death—we had no urge to be buried yet. But death of that which ought to die for the sake of new life. Could we be a living Christian congregation in the future if we did not die to some of the forms and practices of our prior existence which hampered new life? Could we choose death, take it upon ourselves and use it, with its pain, uncertainty, and releasing power? To be masters of our own death—this seemed incredible at first. Can we as men, or as a congregation, really choose our own death and the place where we ought to die? The more we discussed it, the more we decided we were thrown into that choice. We either die ignominiously to no purpose at all, or we stake all on a death we choose deliberately, a death for others.

Thirdly, we affirmed that we are at least partly responsible for our own life as a congregation. This became very clear to us in these three months. Our future was largely in our hands. We could mould it. There came upon us an overpowering sense of the meaning of decision, both personal decision and congregational decision. We are what we decide to be. We knew only too well that decisions are often forgotten, sloughed off, or corrupted. No one had to spend much time giving us a lecture on sin and human frailty. But

14

when the chips were down, as they were in these three months, we knew we could not blame anyone else, or any church structure, or any past history, or any present pressures upon us, for our decisions. We are responsible to take upon and into ourselves the total meaning of our life and make every decision count. Just as we would choose to be caught dead only at the point of significant service to others, we would choose to be caught alive only in the making and execution of decisions wholly consonant with the mission we as individuals and as a congregation undertook as ours. What we would be and do henceforth, insofar as it was humanly possible, would spring from our conscious decision, in line with our most carefully examined intentions in mission.

Finally, we affirmed that we had to know where God is.

You may recall that a stranger was sitting over by the piano, there in our church. He had seemed to be comfortable there. We accepted him. But at some point in those three months, apparently just when we thought some of our purposes were coming clear, he got up and walked out. We wondered about him. He seems to have gone out there in the world some place, probably to be with those others we were discussing. We wished we had listened to what he had tried to say to us. Maybe he would come back—or we might find him out there.

I woke up just as the three months came to an end. The structures we had always known were very much there. No one sensed he had to run away from structure as such. No one regretted those three months. Our lives and our church would never be quite the same again.

I shall always wonder what happened to that congregation. What do you do with a dream?

## THE PURPOSE AND PLAN OF THIS STUDY

The purpose of this study is to explore what it may mean for Christian congregations to participate effectively in God's mission

15

in our twentieth-century world. In the fulfillment of the mission for which God has claimed "a chosen race, a royal priesthood, a dedicated nation" congregational forms and structures are important. Some are helpful and others are not. The search for new congregational forms that will effectively contribute to full and meaningful participation in God's mission must be determined on the one hand by the twentieth-century world in which we live, and our comprehension of it, and on the other hand by the Word given to the world by God in Christ, a Word always open to us under the guidance of the Holy Spirit, particularly as we study the Scriptures. Movement towards new forms which respond adequately to our world and God's Word depends largely on new images and self-concepts which congregations discover for themselves, with mission as the central concern.

The conviction underlying this study is best summed up in the statement that we are ". . . a people claimed by God for his own, to proclaim the triumphs of him who has called you out of darkness into his marvellous light" (I Peter 2:9). In our words, we are claimed by God for mission. God's claim upon us coming out of our history and grasping us as we face the not-yet of our future must be understood ever more deeply by any congregation that seeks to live and serve with relevance in today's world under God's Word.

The steps by which we propose to seek such an understanding are the following:

1. Some present congregational structures can justifiably be called heretical (Chapter I).
2. Many present congregational structures are renewable, provided mission is central to their life (Chapter II).
3. The development of relevant, renewed structures hinges upon our understanding of what God is doing in history (Chapter III).
4. Relevant structures for our twentieth-century world must be

16

responsive to what God is now doing in the midst of dramatic world change (Chapter IV).

5. The development of relevant, renewed structures also depends on their responsiveness to God's Word as recorded in Scripture, which alone gives them ultimate meaning (Chapter V).

6. The search for new congregational forms is aided by the projection of new images that help envisage the goal towards which we may move (Chapter VI).

## chapter I

## HERESY IN OUR MIDST

*Some present congregational structures can justifiably be termed heretical, as they separate the church from its Lord and from its mission, persons from one another, and the gospel from its social implications.*

W E HAVE a great many different ideas about the church, but we can surely agree that the church as we know it is not all it might or should be. Any two persons may find it extremely difficult to agree on what is wrong with the church, but it would be exceedingly hard to find anyone who feels that nothing is wrong with the church. There may have been a time when our forefathers held such a high and holy view of the church that they dared not criticize it for fear of falling into presumptuous sin, but that time has long since gone. Anyone who today would claim that the Christian church is fulfilling its mission in every particular would be written off by all of us as blind to obvious facts or totally ignorant of the gospel, of history, and of what goes on around us.

### THE CHURCH FACES HER CRITICS

Persons outside the church do not hesitate to criticize it. The church is laughed at, rebuked, ridiculed, attacked. Perhaps even worse, it is often ignored. Much of our modern world simply does not take the Christian church into account for anything. It is granted that maybe the church has a "spiritual sphere" with some attraction or meaning for a limited number of individuals, but the world of national and international affairs, of business and hard work, of leisure and delightful friendships—here the church is not present, nor is it wanted. So irrelevant has the church seemed to much of modern life that it is hardly an exaggeration to say that for many the church is simply dead.

It is not only those outside the church who criticize it. The sharpest criticism of the church I have heard has been expressed by church members. Can anyone familiar with church conferences recall a recent meeting on almost any theme that very early in its sessions did not state flatly that the church is a problem? That it is sunk in institutionalism, and that it is in dire need of change, renewal, restructure, and reform? Even the Roman Catholic Church, which many Protestants only recently believed to have lost all capacity for self-criticism, has shown remarkable insight into its own failings, as Vatican II amply testifies. Those who know the church best, from the inside, appear to be its strongest critics.

Much of the prevalent criticism arises from what one observer has called "a reservoir of creative discontent." If it is genuinely creative, we can all be grateful for it. If it is merely destructive, offering no alternative but the criticism itself, it is only worthwhile if one accepts the premise that it is better to have no church at all than to have the very imperfect church we generally encounter. Some friends of mine take this latter position. I reject it. I share many of the criticisms of the local congregation as we know it but only because I believe they may serve to prepare the way for a movement towards more faithful congregations.

When, some years ago, we were demolishing an old building in Uruguay that had to be razed to make way for a new church edifice, we greatly enjoyed watching the demolition. When the demolition concluded, however, we had nothing left but a bare piece of land. The major and most important task was still ahead. Our concern here is not one of demolition for its own sake. Rather we want to seek outlet channels for this "reservoir of creative discontent."

Something is wrong with the church. What that something is may not be so easy to identify. Is the church too identified with the world or too separate from it? Is it too secular or too saintly? Is it over-organized or too disorganized? Is it too moralistic or too immoral? Is it too sophisticated or too naive?

The variety of criticisms is overwhelming and also disconcerting. A casual listener comes inevitably to the conclusion that a study would be in order to determine the roots and validity of the criticisms of the church. Hopefully this study might isolate some of the major failings of the church which an imaginative program could attack and overcome. This sounds logical, even simple. Deceptively so. It has been tried and tried, again and again, and agreement still remains distant.

## STUDIES OF STRUCTURE

The New Delhi Assembly of the World Council of Churches in 1961 set in motion just the sort of study suggested above, not as some definitive, once-and-for-all solution, but as another step in man's quest to understand himself in relation to the church. It is really a search for the meaning of God's activity in human history, which in part at least is carried on in relationship to the body called the church. The title of the World Council of Churches study is "The Missionary Structure of the Congregation."

It may be that this title is too vague. What is meant by the terms "missionary," "structure," and "congregation"? Groups that have attempted this study have quickly bogged down in a morass of definitions that, in the end, have apparently hindered rather than helped their search for the inner meaning of the theme.

Attempts have been made to restate the theme. The study book for East Asian churches rephrases the title this way: *Structures for a Missionary Congregtaion,* with a subtitle, "The Shape of the Christian Community in Asia Today." Colin Williams' book,

*Where in the World?* [1] has a subtitle that also attempts to get at the meaning of the World Council theme: "Changing Forms of the Church's Witness." It seems that no one phrase fully expresses the concept towards which "the missionary structure of the congregation" points. The concern of all is the means used by a group to serve as a channel for the expression and fulfillment of its mission.

The danger of concentration on structure and machinery is very real. This is particularly the case if our emphasis is on the "efficiency" of a "smooth-running" organization which produces "results" that can be "reported" at some "conference." Presumably the group came together originally for a laudable purpose. A task had to be accomplished. Concentration on the means to achieve the task all too easily can deviate attention from the purposes that at one time gave life to the group. Therefore let it be said at the outset that the reason for the study of "the missionary structure of the congregation" is precisely to get away from any suggestion that one more organizational pattern might be a panacea for our ills. It seeks rather to focus attention on the mission, that for which the church exists at all, and in so doing to seek "forms," "shapes," and "structures" of the widest variety that may contribute to the fulfillment of that mission. The clear assumption is that the end must determine the means. The purpose for which the church lives and moves and has its being, is its mission. Everything else in the congregation depends on this.

A most intriguing question for the Christian church today is whether the forms it employs to carry on its work are in any sense heretical.

## HERESY AND HERETICAL FORMS

Our tolerant twentieth-century minds do not take kindly to the word "heresy." Heresy smacks of closed intellects of other ages

---

[1] Colin Williams, *Where in the World?* National Council of the Churches of Christ in the U.S.A., 1963.

22

that insisted too strenuously on a pure and orthodox doctrine from which no deviation was permitted. It calls to mind fiery deaths at the stake of men and women who dared to differ with the preservers of "correct" ideas. In our imagination we see the fanatic on a witch hunt, zealous to bludgeon everyone into line with his fanatically held frame of thought.

History books tell us of periods when the issues between orthodoxy and heresy were the central concern of a community or a nation. Men argued, fought, and died over doctrinal points we scarcely comprehend. All this seems strange to our "democratic way of thought." We live in a pluralistic society. We assume that wide differences of opinions do and should exist. Our nation has developed political, administrative, and judicial means by which we channel, arbitrate, and settle major differences among us in order to insure a reasonable order and tranquility. We do not set out consciously to eliminate our differences. "Live and let live" is our slogan. The word "heresy" is not a part of our daily vocabulary.

To be sure, some of us have been brought up short in our complacency in this regard when we have witnessed in our own lifetime too many examples of what could fairly be described as the persecution of heresy. Modern totalitarian governments insist on adherence to the party line, and they banish dissent. In our own land, even to mention "McCarthyism" is to recall a whole mind-set that captured much of our country less than two decades ago. It set out to destroy the reputations of men who did not espouse the proper ideas and principles of the "American way of life" in the same way as their inquisitors did. To dissent from the opinions of these inquisitors was to be "heretical." There was the threat of loss of job, reputation, and future. We witness something akin to this today in communities which effectively maintain a particular stance regarding some social cause.

Community pressure impinges strongly on persons whose actions or statements differ from the viewpoint commonly accepted by the

23

majority. Threatening telephone calls disturb sleep, homemade bombs destroy property, or the "heretic" is simply frozen out of the community by social ostracism and determined opposition. Heresy, by whatever name, is still very much with us.

Webster gives two definitions of heresy. First, it is "religious opinion opposed to the authorized doctrinal standards of any particular church, and tending to promote schism." Second, it is "an opinion held in opposition to the commonly received doctrine, and tending to promote division or dissension." The first definition emphasizes the religious character of heresy. The second extends the concept to differing opinions, whether or not they refer to what we usually ascribe to the religious realm. In both cases the end result is separation, division, dissension.

What does this suggest for us as we consider the forms of congregational life our church has developed to carry on its task? Though the idea of heresy generally refers to the realm of ideas, doctrines, and opinions (as Webster's definitions indicate), may we not usefully employ the concept of heresy as an analytical tool in examining the forms and structures which our church uses to further its task? [2]

## SEPARATION FROM CHRIST

In the first place, *a heretical structure is one which tends to separate the church from its Lord*. The relationship between the Christian church and Christ Jesus its Lord is so intimate that Biblical imagery presents a wide variety of pictures designed to show the inextricable link between them. We mention but two. The Lord is the "bridegroom," and the church is "the bride of Christ." The intimacy of the marriage relationship is recalled. Each partner gives himself fully to the other in bodily and spiritual unity. Another is that of Christ as the "head of the church" and the church as "the

---

[2] Colin Williams reminds us that the concept of "heretical structures" within the World Council of Churches study arose in the Western European Working Group, and subsequently received considerable attention there.

body of Christ." Here the unity is even more evident. Without the head the body cannot exist. It dies. It is incomplete and lifeless.

At stake in these images in the Lord's sovereignty. For us as a church, is Christ the Lord or not? We like to think that he is, but our thoughts and feelings are largely irrelevant at this point. If his sovereignty implies an unconditional dominion over our lives, our church, our time, and our possessions, certain results have to follow. It is not difficult to point to forms by which we interpose blocks to such sovereignty. They separate us from our Lord. They are heretical structures.

Take, for instance, the matter of time. What structures in an average congregation require a particular use of time which might separate the participants in that congregation from their Lord? At the 1964 Methodist General Conference in Pittsburgh one evening's presentation was given over to a words-and-music drama complete with modern dance and a jazz combo. It endeavored to analyze some of the ills of our modern church. The theme was church renewal. How can the church be renewed? Dramatically the question became entangled with pressing concerns that pushed aside the essential reasons for the existence of the church. There is a leaky roof that must be fixed. There is a church supper that will break the backs of industrious ladies. Throughout the song recurs, "You gotta do church work!" Time gets preempted by "church work." And you "gotta" do it.

The church sets up a wide gamut of time-consuming structures that exact work from its members which may or may not be related even remotely to an acknowledgment of the sovereignty of Jesus Christ in the life of the congregation or the community. We will give endless hours to a building committee to discuss the shape of a building or the color of a drape. ("The church needs a good building, doesn't it?") But we seldom have similar time for intent analysis with fellow Christians of the implications of the message which we

25

hope will some day be proclaimed in the new building. We sew and knit and bake for the charity bazaar. ("It is for a good cause, isn't it? And think of all the good fellowship we have while we knock ourselves out doing it.") But we have little time to participate in a controversial community activity that might witness to Christ's Lordship in our town—perhaps a meeting with our neighbors to help elect a more effective school board.

The limited time we possess is often captured by the congregation for tasks that may be important and may do some good. But too often they are marginal to the major reasons for which the church exists in the first place. Far from participation in the glorious drama of salvation, they are reductions to "church work"—rather pointless, time-filling, routine. This is heresy. The structures that encourage and provide for this separate the church and its people from their Lord. The sovereignty of the Lord is replaced by the sovereignty of whatever time-consuming work is at hand. This is not to say that many routine tasks should not be done. Many have their real significance. The issue, however, is whether our congregational structures can move us towards a consideration of first priorities required by the Lord's sovereignty over our church.

First priorities! Here would seem to be a primary need for a congregation that wants to be faithful: to sit down as a congregation (or as an official board, committee, or group of friends) to analyze what our major purposes are. One of the largest and most flourishing churches in Methodism, which probably has as many activities going per square foot (and square head!) as any congregation, recently decided this was a way to begin again.[3]

In an orderly yet persistent manner this church set out over a two-year period to ask three basic questions. The first was, What are our major purposes as a Christian congregation? The senior minister told me that the answer to this question should not be difficult to

---

[3] The excellent study referred to is entitled ". . . *To the Limit of Our Vision*," prepared by the Highland Park Methodist Church, Dallas, Texas, 1965.

formulate because our charter is given in the New Testament. But our understanding of the New Testament is quite something else, and we do not simply quote the Bible and jump to the conclusion that these are *our* major concerns. Each congregation has to reappropriate this faith for itself and understand it in the terms of that congregation.

Thus a faithful church—one that aims to maintain an intimate and close relationship between the God revealed in Jesus Christ and its congregational life—decides consciously, in the face of hell, high water, and countless activities, to give major attention to the basic reasons for which it lives. In time it will probably want to write out on paper: "The Gospel According to ——————————" (inserting the name of the congregation), a gospel that later understanding might change but which for the moment is *our* charter in which *our* fundamental aims and understandings are hammered out.

This is no easy task. It demands decision, time, interaction of many ideas, serious discussion, drafts and redrafts, and above all, searching Biblical study. Once done, however, or at least once well commenced, the second and third questions formulated by the congregation mentioned above can be tackled with relevance and meaning, namely, (1) Where are we now, as a congregation, in relation to our major purposes? and (2) What specific steps, in line with our purposes, must be taken to move from our present position to a place more in harmony with our stated aims?

## SEPARATION FROM THE MISSION

Second, *a heretical structure is one which tends to separate the church from its mission.* God defines the mission for us. We may not understand it in all its complexity, but we do know that the church does not exist simply to be an island unto itself. It has tasks to accomplish out beyond itself. The congregation gathers to reaffirm its allegiance to its Lord, to worship him, to study its task, to share in the "communion of the saints." It may even enjoy itself when it does these things! But if this is as far as it gets, it has developed what quite properly has been described as a "come structure." People come together as a congregation for laudable or questionable purposes. They may sense some kind of "oneness" and thrill to the "fellowship." If it ends there, no matter what goes on in that coming together, it is heretical. For the purpose of a congregation's gathering should always be preparation for mission. The frontier of mission is out beyond the congregational group in the world of family, business, political action, national and international life. The arena of mission is where faith meets unfaith. It is most often encountered by the Christian when he is not with his fellow churchmen. The group scatters, each member of it to work out his own Christian life and witness in the intricacies of daily living.

The scattered church, infiltrated in the crevices of society, is no less the church than the gathered congregation in the hospitable sanctuary. The gathered church without mission is not a Christian church at all. It is a heretical club.

Recently I read a most interesting report from a missionary in North Africa. Traditionally North Africa has been considered by Methodist missionaries as the toughest spot on earth to be a Christian missionary. In our day it is not so easy to single out a particular area as especially rugged, since merely to call the names of Cuba, Congo, China, or Indonesia reminds us that witness to Jesus Christ is apt to be exacting business anywhere in the world. The problem in North Africa is the tight opposition of Islam. Conversions come hard, if they come at all. Missionary work is "hard-scrabble," as one man put it. So what is the attitude of the tiny Christian church there to be? I gathered from the report I read that many Christians in the past saw the role of the church to be somewhat like a grueling assault on an entrenched bastion to conquer some souls who would be brought back alive to the fold of the church. D. T. Niles has described this as "Noah's Ark Evangelism," bringing the animals back into the ark for fellowship with the rest of us! One need hardly add that such a conception is in no way limited to North Africa. The report, however, went on to plead for an entirely new attitude. Far from the defensiveness which is the antithesis of love, let us converse with eagerness in whatever dialogue is possible. In a word, turn the church outward to the world at its door. Meet Christ who roams the world "out there" and is never grasped by any tight circle of baptized elite. Openness makes the church itself open to mission.

Worship that may be beautiful but irrelevant to the seven-day-a-week witness service of the worshipers is heretical. It separates the congregation from its mission. A sermon that forgets the wide world of need and human conflict to concentrate on personal, individual salvation alone is heretical: it separates man from his mission in the world. In effect the church *is* mission, or it is not the Christian church. A faithful congregation knows itself to be constrained by mission. Its every structure is demanded by its mission.

## SEPARATION BETWEEN CHURCHMEN

Third, *a heretical structure is one that tends to separate persons within the church from each other*. A colleague of mine, now a missionary in Latin America, remembers one of his first parishes in the Southwest. He was forewarned that a split had developed in the congregation to the point where the two sides were hardly speaking to each other. His first introduction to the congregation was a "welcome" supper at which one faction sat on one side of the church hall and the other group sat on the opposite side. My friend and his wife were at a special table in the center, equidistant from both sides! His task was cut out for him: to reunite a broken congregation. The walls of separation which exist in our Christian churches are usually far less evident than this. Barriers are erected in silence, divisions pass unnoticed, destructive comments are couched in genteel phrases, social pressures that include some and exclude others are seldom discussed.

The Methodist Church has struggled for decades with the problem of its Central Jurisdiction. At the time of Methodist union in 1939 The Methodist Church was organized into five geographical jurisdictions and a sixth non-geographical jurisdiction, the Central Jurisdiction, which included most of the "Negro" churches. Whatever the validity or expediency of this arrangement—and exceedingly strong arguments are marshalled in its defence—the fact was that a well-defined ecclesiastical structure was set up which separated Negro churches in one organizational arrangement and white churches in another. Within one and the same Methodist Church a carefully worked out structure separated persons of one color from persons of another. It is to the credit of The Methodist Church that since the very inception of this arrangement strenuous efforts have been made towards the elimination of the Central Jurisdiction, and already in many parts of the nation it no longer exists.

The implications of this elimination still remain to be faced. Recently I sat in a quarterly conference of a Northern all-white congregation. The discussion centered around the question: will this congregation accept any minister regardless of race? Previously the existence of the Central Jurisdiction made it practically certain that no Negro would be appointed as minister of that church. In this area the Central Jurisdiction has been abolished. Now any minister in that conference, whatever his color, might be appointed by the bishop to any church in the area. Did this congregation accept this fact in its full force? In absolute frankness many members did not. For a multitude of reasons they would prefer to maintain an arrangement which would insure that this congregation would be served by a white minister. Others differed, welcoming any competent minister. The word "heresy" was not used, but the attraction of a heretical structure which would separate some persons from others in that congregation was evident.

The Lord's Supper is a sacrament supremely fitted for reconciliation. It is itself a structure—instituted by our Lord—which a faithful congregation observes periodically. We are invited to participate with the initial words, "Ye that do truly and earnestly repent of your sins, and are in love and charity with your neighbors . . ." All barriers are down. We join each other and "with angels and archangels, and with all the company of heaven" we praise God. We receive symbols of the body and blood of our Lord Jesus Christ and enter into a renewed unity with him and with our neighbor.

In February, 1964, I was privileged to travel to Cuba. With the permission of the United States and Cuban governments three of us went to visit the Methodist church there. We experienced a memorable week as we saw firsthand the faithful witness of a church sorely tried by tremendously difficult political circumstances. For me the high point of the week was a home communion service.

A large Havana church, in addition to its regularly scheduled services, holds informal weekly home meetings in various sections of the city. I asked if I might attend one and was cordially welcomed. About twenty of us crowded into the home of a Methodist layman, while two armed militiamen stood at the door. (We never did find out just why they were there, but the meeting went on unhindered.) This layman had faced the death of his wife only weeks before. I expected this would be a home shrouded in tragedy but found it to be a place of serene and deep-seated Christian faith and joy. Gathered there (I was told later) were some who were quite favorable to Fidel Castro's revolution and others deeply opposed to it. The meeting began with conversation about the topics of most interest to the group—food rationing, a child who would be operated on the next day, the problems some faced in their daily jobs. A young minister's wife played an accordion, and we sang some favorite hymns. There was a period of prayer, and finally all was gathered up into a simple yet deeply moving communion service. The same symbolic elements were passed out to Cubans and to a U. S. citizen, to defenders and opponents of Fidel Castro, to Negroes and whites, to children and adults. In that moment we were one in Christ. A faithful congregation gave witness that divisive structures out beyond the church would not divide those who worshipped Jesus Christ and knew themselves to be part of his body.

## SEPARATION OF THE GOSPEL FROM ITS IMPLICATIONS

Fourth, *a heretical structure is one which tends to separate the proclamation of the gospel from the implications of that gospel for a Christian's life in society*. Subtle yet very real separations are established between the Word of God and the work of man. As individuals, if we are honest, we recognize that every one of us is guilty of this sin. We say one thing and do another. We mouth the Sermon on the Mount and draw little if any relation between it and daily business. After all, "business is business." We celebrate the Cross and give thanks that Jesus died for all men, but we act as though some men are intrinsically better than others because of their ancestry or their income. We ask God to "forgive us our trespasses as we forgive those who trespass against us," but we nurture the hurts we have received and refuse to give them up or reconcile our relationship with the one who trespassed on our pride.

In the collective life of the church such a separation between word and work is less evident but no less real. The church proclaims God as Creator of all men, but often all men cannot freely enter temples erected to the worship of that same God or become members of the congregation that proclaims such truths. A congregation gradually surrounded by slums of the inner city intones, "Blessed are the poor," while concurrently it endeavors to flee from the area of the poor to suffer the soporific comforts of suburban captivity.

Few verses of Scripture are more dear to the church than "Go therefore and make disciples of all nations . . ." Yet more often than not congregations will build into their budgets year after year arrangements by which far more will be spent on care and maintenance of the church building and parsonage than will be invested in the missionary enterprise of the church either at home or abroad. Heresy in structure finds no better outlet than to obscure sub-Christian practices with the fog of familiar Christian phrases to which all of us readily assent.

In most of Latin America one of the greatest social curses is the national lottery. As extensions of legalized gambling and state lotteries are proposed in the United States, one wishes more people might see something of the family devastation, the poverty, and the twisted values produced across Latin America by such schemes. Early in my ministry in Uruguay several young persons in our tiny congregation resolved they should write a brief statement stating clearly their opposition to legalized gambling on the basis of the Christian faith. This was done in the form of a letter to the editor of the local paper. We made it very clear that anyone who signed the letter might suffer certain repercussions. Somewhat fearful, several preferred not to sign. About ten persons did. The letter was published. The first repercussion came when a young girl, employed in a dry goods store, and still quite new in her Protestant Christian faith, came to me highly disturbed because her employer threatened to fire her from her job because she had signed such a statement. The employer, she assured me, was almost hysterical. Then the girl added, "If I had known this might happen, I certainly would not have signed that letter!"

It takes time for a new Christian to discover the implications of Christian faith for life in our kind of world. It takes time, and effort as well, for a congregation to work out a harmony between its proclaimed faith and the life it lives in society. A faithful congregation finds that such time and effort are well spent.

The church may have to change radically if it is to be faithful to Jesus Christ. In many areas, we must admit, congregations as we know them are less than faithful. We rejoice in the belief, however, that faithful structures are within our reach and that a renewal of

33

congregational life in our day may well flow from the prevalent "reservoir of creative discontent."

\* \* \*

## Questions for Discussion

1. What are the most important characteristics of a missionary congregation?
2. As you think of the local congregation to which you belong, what goes to make up its "missionary structure"?
3. What structures in the congregation tend to place a barrier between the members of the congregation and the Lord of the congregation?
4. Is it possible for a Christian congregation to be a non-missionary congregation?
5. In your community, what specific social implications of the gospel are crucial for a congregation to take seriously?

## chapter II

## THE LOCAL CONGREGATION—A SOURCE OF HOPE

*Many present congregational structures are renewable, provided mission is central to their life: a mission that is comprehensive, open to the future, and intentionalistic.*

A GROWING CONCERN among many church leaders, both clergy and laymen, is that present church structures are something of a straight-jacket that cramps the style and freedom of anyone who is serious about church renewal. In a word, many of our present structures may already be heretical.

A bishop reports that able young men are increasingly shying away from the pastoral ministry, not out of any lack of Christian commitment nor out of fear of what daily seems to be a more difficult job, but simply because they do not want to get enmeshed in a "system" that will hamper creativity and will demand endless work and time devoted mainly to keep the "system" going.

A seminary reports that its students in ever larger percentages do not want to commit themselves to any structure that will force them into rigid ecclesiastical patterns that seem to be quite stale. Therefore they seek other channels for expression of their Christian vocation, such as teaching in colleges or universities, or in newly developing Christian movements or communities which appear to be sufficiently flexible for experimentation and the development of appealing and meaningful forms of Christian witness.

## CRITICISM CAN HELP

A former Methodist missionary back in the United States wrote not long ago: "We feel totally dissatisfied with the present structures as a base to work towards renewal and reform. Many, many others are expressing the same conviction, privately and publicly. I think before we came here we still felt it was feasible to start as a professional worker, with a fulltime responsibility in the present structures, and simultaneously to work towards new patterns for the renewal of the church. For me at least, I no longer feel this can be done." He pulled out of missionary service overseas and eventually purchased an independent business to start out on the road of a concerned Christian layman who simply cannot see much hope for renewal or reform within the organized church he has known, either at home or overseas.

Gordon Cosby, founder and pastor of the creative experimental Church of the Saviour in Washington, D.C., has come to a somewhat similar conclusion. In a sermon entitled "The Charismatic Community," preached in December 1962, he squarely faces the fact that the Christian church exists as a minority people. We have to give up the "myth of Christendom because there is no longer any Christendom." Then he forcefully states this conviction:

The church as we know it in our time must go. This conviction has come to me gradually—I have worked with it consciously for the past 15 years and have been disturbed about it for the past three. Just a few weeks ago I crossed a line in my thinking. Now I am on the side of feeling that the institutional structures that we know are not renewable. Even when there is renewal (and this goes on in many congregations) the stance of the church almost always remains the same—a stance which is contrary to the very nature of a church committed to mission.

The church, properly, doesn't engage in mission or merely send missionaries—the church IS mission and the congregation should express its life in the world. Its very structure must be changed to allow it to be itself.

Of course there will be a coming, and a gathering, and the *koinonia*. But the church, if it is to 'go into all nations', must exist within the secular structures of mankind.

When the structures get as rigid and as resistant to changes as they are now, perhaps the wisest strategy is not to try to renew or to reform these structures through which the church expresses its life. It may be wiser strategy to bypass them and let God do with them what he will. But what happens will have to be so drastic that it would be reform rather than renewal. The basic direction and the basic shape must be different.

I would suggest that those of us who are called by the living God to belong to Him will be on mission to His world and we will take the shape appropriate to our calling. This in itself will give a light to the old structures.

Many statements could be added to this chorus of dissatisfaction with the church structures as they are presently constituted and in operation.

Those of us who work within present church structures should recognize (1) that this protest is sincere, (2) that it is widespread, and (3) that it is creative. We would seriously misunderstand its intent and power if we were to write it off as simply the protest of a small minority unaware of the realities of life, immature because it rebels at the acceptance of responsibilities structures impose.

Above all, this protest is necessary in this day for the life of the church itself. Thoughtful critics hold the established church structures under a judgment that the church dare not ignore. Creative experimentation out beyond traditional patterns of church life and organization should be welcomed because aside from its intrinsic value and service it may well constitute a pioneering which will indicate ways in which the church may be more faithful to its mission and its Lord.

The point at which we must object is at the suggestion that the *only* possible place for the concerned Christian to work is outside present church structures. Without minimizing the excellent Christian witness possible beyond traditional church forms, I believe there still remains ample opportunity within most churches as now constituted for a vibrant and vital Christian witness. Traditional congregations can be renewed; they can find avenues of faithfulness within present structures; and they can reform the structure themselves, from the inside, in order that the church may be more faithful in its witness. To some this may seem hopelessly defensive and traditionalistic. I do not believe it is. I would not minimize for a moment the drag of bureaucratic institutionalism, the ponderous movement of large denominational bodies, the frustrations of a modern pastor harried by reports and more reports that seem fruitless and unnecessary, the thousand and one ways in which fresh and creative ideas get stifled by committee machinery or by stodgy leadership. Yet in spite of this I believe that renewal of most local congregations is possible, a renewal which will encompass both the life of the church and the forms it uses to express its life as well.

An outstanding example of the possibility of renewal from the inside has become evident to all the world from a source which only a few years back would have seemed one of the least likely candidates among church structures for any kind of significant change, namely, the Roman Catholic Church. Here was a traditional church, burdened down with centuries of established doctrine and practice, which suddenly surprised the world, including most persons within the Roman church itself, with a burst of renewal that could not have been predicted or anticipated by anyone. One need not wait for a final judgment on the Second Vatican Council to assert that the course taken by Pope John XXIII opened up vast new channels of creativity within the church and that the very *aggiornamento* (bringing the church up to date) he propounded has brought the church into the twentieth century with vigor and a new intellectual honesty that will have lasting effects. Unquestionably there existed within the Roman Catholic Church a great "reservoir of creative discontent" which needed a rallying point and a channel. This was provided by Pope John XXIII. If this can happen within the Roman Catholic Church, may not renewal and reform be possible within present-day Protestant churches? I believe that similar longings exist among us and that they can be tapped for significant breakthroughs in church life and Christian witness.

## Two Examples of Renewal

A Christian urban center in Buenos Aires challenges the church in Argentina to take seriously its responsibility to great population centers while concomitantly it experiments with new forms of ministry. It studies what structures the church might use to minister more effectively to urban life. The center is unconventional and unpredictable. It displays no impressive statistics. It raises more questions than it answers. Some within the established church structure write it off as a temporary and illusory venture. But the center continues in its work, an integral part of the church structure in Argentina, probing, analyzing, challenging.

A Methodist church in Cleveland, Ohio, seeks a recovery of relevance in that great city. The congregation organized "*koinonia* groups," fellowship groups centered on Biblical study. The groups were made up of concerned laymen, many of them dissatisfied with conventional Christianity as they have previously known it. They agree upon a discipline of regular worship, daily prayer, personal and group Bible study, regular commitment of time and money to the ongoing mission of the congregation, and witness in daily work and community life. They are a leaven in helping one community to face up squarely to the implications and the opportunities of racial integration. Genuine new life and witness moves through that congregation. It questions many church structures and refashions some of them for its purposes. Yet it remains within the broad established church framework, convinced that its most effective job of renewal and reform can be carried on from the inside.

The important feature to be noted in these examples is not simply that new life and meaning may be found within traditional structures. It is rather the primary concern for the mission of the church and of the individuals who compose the congregation. What describes the renewed congregation is a basic concern for the mission that God calls the church to perform. If a congregation takes seriously its endeavor to understand what God's mission is, it is not fundamentally important whether old or new forms are used, provided they serve to advance the mission and do not get in the way of it. To say that only new and previously untried forms can be used is to close our eyes to the many ways in which, even in our day, older structures are being widely and wisely used for participation in God's purposes.

### THREE CHARACTERISTICS OF A CHRISTIAN CONGREGATION

I attended a most stimulating weekend institute held recently at the Ecumenical Institute in Chicago, Illinois. The theme was the renewal of a modern local congregation. As part of the initial presentation a Christian man of faith was described as comprehensive, open to the future, and intentionalistic. The meaning of this description needs probing. As we think of the mission of the church, which is the central matter of concern for any congregation, what does it mean that a Christian group should be comprehensive, open to the future, and intentionalistic? Let us take each quality in turn.

First, *a Christian congregation is comprehensive.* Perhaps the easiest attitude of mind for anyone to fall into is that of self-concern. An individual may extend that concern to those persons and matters closely related to him: his family, his business responsibilities, his house and lawn, his neighbors, his town. A congregation may find this self-concern, somewhat expanded, is typical of its group life as well. The congregation is likely to give major attention to its membership, its program, its worship services, its organizations, some aspects of local community life. No person or congregation is totally self-concerned, but the pattern of self-interest is admittedly easy to fall into. Yet the Christian man and the Christian congregation, if they think seriously about the mission to which God calls them, will immediately recognize that the limits of their concern must be pushed out to include ever greater circles of interest and responsibility.

A congregation cannot grow in self-understanding and in understanding of the mission of God without soon asking itself what its mission is to the complex community that surrounds it. All the groupings, tensions, communication opportunities, and business pressures in the community are matters of concern. Beyond the local community are national issues and problems of vital import. And further still, the immense world of nations and power groups around the globe are ultimately within the concern of the church, and these are the concerns not just of some large, ethereal, ecumenical church, but of the local congregation. To be comprehensive is to affirm a responsibility for the whole gamut of man's world. Comprehensiveness is the opposite of narrow parochialism and limited self-concern.

The comprehensive concern of the congregation needs to be emphasized in a day such as this. We are discovering the centrality of mission to the life of the Christian congregation, but we stand in danger of limiting mission to that which is nearest to us. We can be thankful that the day has gone when mission was something occurring only across the seas in some far distant land. We know that mission is on our very doorstep, and we are called to mission here and now. Every one of us is called in this sense to be a missionary.

The local congregation cannot escape its doorstep mission by giving money for a missionary in Japan or Rhodesia. But the reverse is equally true. Because we recognize that mission is at our doorstep, we dare not forget the vast mission field which is beyond our immediate vision but which is as much a portion of our Christian responsibility as what is closer and more obvious. Christian comprehensiveness requires it. Douglas Webster in his little book *Local Church and World Mission* puts it succinctly by saying: "This means that every local congregation has to be made profoundly and disturbingly aware of what is happening in the whole world and in the whole Church." [1]

Max Warren makes essentially the same point: "This is one world, and that responsibility for what is on our own doorstep can only be fully discharged in the context of our own responsibility for those further away." [2]

When I first decided to go to South America as a Methodist missionary, a very able District Superintendent strongly urged against it. He argued that, though undoubtedly there was much for the Christian church to do in Latin America, we were in a period of rediscovering that we had a mission at home and that it was surely at least of equal importance. Why travel six thousand miles? He had a point. I could not claim that the mission in which I would participate in Uruguay was more important than the one in which he was engaged at home. I did feel then, and still feel, that his argument lacked a sense of Christian comprehensiveness; for ultimately his concern with a district in the United States had to include the farthest bounds of the world itself. It is difficult to understand how any congregation seriously concerned about its mission can fail to seek out channels for the expression of a wide concern for the world at large, through prayer, study, giving, and whatever service it can offer. However crucial the mission at our fingertips, it should never undermine the ever widening comprehensive Christian concern for God's mission to the ends of the earth.

Second, *a Christian congregation is open to the future.* To my mind, openness to the future has to do on the one hand with insecurities and on the other with proper questioning. First, insecur-

---

[1] Douglas Webster, *Local Church and World Mission*, The Seabury Press, New York, 1964, page 9.
[2] Max Warren, *Perspective in Mission*, The Seabury Press, New York, 1964, page 18.

ities. Nothing seems more secure than the past. We know what it has been, and we feel confident it will not change. We look towards the past to find our immovable bases, our secure foundations. One of the true functions of a Christian church is to look to the past and transmit into the present a sense of the major securities of life. There are rocks of faith that we trust. The church preserves in its tradition the glories of Christian history, and rightly so. But no church can live exclusively by its past; and every time it attempts such a thing, it signals its own decay and ineffectiveness. Mission comes to the church out of the future, and this means that we are called as individuals and as a congregation into ground quite insecure.

A young student pastor undertook to provide a weekend ministry to children in a Long Island orphanage. The boys and girls had come from broken homes. Many had been mistreated and abandoned. It was no easy matter for them to sense the meaning of love in human relationships. The student pastor described his experiences: "I know I have a mission to these kids. I feel very much alone in it. No one else seems to care. These kids do not respond as others do. I never know what will happen next. I feel totally insecure. By the end of each weekend I threaten never to return again. But so far I have always gone back." The Christian congregation can have no more security than that if it really gets involved in thorny community issues, if it takes a stand that contravenes generally accepted community opinions, or if it plunges into an inner city where it is generally unwanted, often ignored, sometimes hated. No congregation moves into the future, out ahead of those groups that cherish peace and comfort, without venturing into extremely insecure ground which might well conceal a cross—and the Cross is the ultimate in insecurity.

The area of insecurity is increasingly familiar to those who know something about the life of the church around the world. If a missionary candidate gives indication that he wishes to be a missionary but hopes he may be sent to some place that is fairly stable and secure, where can he go today? There is no such place. He must know that wherever he goes he probably will not be wanted there by most persons around him. He will be resented, envied, challenged, tricked, laughed at, molested. Secondary securities, such as praise of friends, pride in accomplishment, support by colleagues, and evidence of results may all drop away and vanish. His mission compels him into insecurity. Either he learns to live in the middle of the insecurity, or he will eventually find reasons to withdraw from further missionary service. The point is that mission, which moves into uncharted areas of the future, inevitably thrusts us out into insecurity.

The other aspect of openness to the future is that it obligates a congregation to ask some searching questions. John Heuss, in a much published essay on "The True Function of a Christian Church" suggests that in every parish "a revolutionary thing can be done." He describes it this way:

I believe there needs to be some thoughtful group made up of laymen and women in every parish which has the responsibility of asking three questions and finding the answers to them:

First, what is the true religious job of this parish? Second, how can all that is done in this whole parish set forward that true religious task? Third, to what extent is everything which we are doing changing the lives of the people involved?

In the average local church, nobody ever asks these basic questions. It is generally assumed by the lay people that this is something the pastor is taking care of. Yet, it is not possible for him to do it by himself. If he is the only one caring and thinking about it, it will never happen.

The necessity of asking searching questions is not felt by those who live solely in the past or in the present. It is only as a congregation begins to project itself into the future and tries to fathom what its mission really is that basic questions get asked and tentative answers begin to appear. The measure of a Christian congregation's ability to deal with the future is often found in the quality and depth of the questions with which it wrestles. Any local congregation can begin that questioning today.

Take but one large question some congregations are beginning to consider. It is this: Should a congregation be structured mainly along residential lines, or are there other factors that should bring a congregation into existence? Most congregations have never faced this question. Yet today an increasing volume of thoughtful writing is raising this issue in a most challenging way.[3] Most of our congregational life is structured along residence patterns. We attend the church near our home, or we travel some distance to attend a church the members of which live in homes such as ours, which means they usually belong to a similar economic and social grouping. Do the congregations of the future have to continue this pattern? Should they? Is there not some possibility, even probability, of socio-economic separation implicit in this pattern? Does it not belie the inclusiveness of the Christian community? Are there not other groupings from which Christian congregational life is virtually absent and in which new congregational forms should be sought, such as in professional and labor groups, business communities, and other areas of public life? Easy answers to such questions are not forthcoming. A congregation open to the future does not flinch, however, at asking them and seeking out tentative replies upon which it initiates appropriate action.

Implicit in the question about residential congregations is the larger question regarding the proper sphere of a congregation. A group related principally to residence is most likely to deal with individual and family concerns. These are very present and press-

---

[3] See Colin Williams, *op. cit.*, also *What in the World?*, National Council of the Churches of Christ in the U.S.A , 1964; Gibson Winter, *The Suburban Captivity of the Churches*, Doubleday, 1961; Harvey Cox, *The Secular City*, The Macmillan Company, 1965.

ing matters of interest. The Christian church is very properly called upon to help deal with the complications and frustrations of our inner spiritual life, our fears and guilts, our personal sins and our hidden ambitions. We know very well it should be present at the points of crisis in life: birth, marriage, illness, tragedy, death. We expect it to have something to contribute to our family life, to the education of our children, and to the maintenance of a happy home. We may even expect it to give us some guidelines about the proper role of a citizen in a local community, though particular responsibilities often become a bit hazy. All these areas are closely tied to our residence. They are of vital concern and quite properly a sphere of interest and activity for a Christian congregation.

But many other areas of life in our modern world are not closely tied to a place of residence. This is especially the case in urban centers with regard to the work of employed men and women. More often than not, in the city a man's place of work is not located in the immediate neighborhood where he lives. Daily he "leaves home" to "go to work" in some distant place. He commutes "from home to work." The church he attends on Sunday is close to his home. If there is a church building located near his place of business, it is generally not *his* church. What is more, neither the church near his home nor the church near his place of work accepts responsibility for ministering to him in the midst of his work. The one area to which the man gives the most concentrated attention of his waking hours and upon which his entire livelihood depends apparently is, for the church, a marginal concern. Congregations open to the future will ask themselves whether they might develop the means by which Christians engaged in similar vocational pursuits may come together to submit their work life to the scrutiny of the gospel. This may well mean the development of new groupings, new congregations, that may bring to bear Christian insight and wisdom upon business life in a way that residential congregations are seldom able to do.

Third, *a Christian congregation is intentionalistic.* This is to say that it does not allow itself to be the victim of sheer chance or circumstance and drift along without some sense of intention and direction. A missionary congregation takes upon itself, by a conscious decision, the mission God places upon it. The problem, of course, is that no congregation can easily know what precisely is God's mission, nor exactly how to participate in it. The congregation is thrown into a continual crisis of decision as to where, to be faithful, it must make its intentions known both to itself and to others. It lives by repeated and unending decisions to be what by God's grace it can be: an agent of his mission in the world. The tragedy of so much congregational life is that decisions of this import are seldom faced. Many congregations go on from year to year following pretty much the same patterns and programs they have known. They never face the crisis of decision, they neither experience the agony of uncertainty nor accept the opportunity of significant involvement in some vital part of God's mission. The Christian congregation alive to its mission knows that it must decide, and that to some degree it fashions by its decisions its own future and the future of the world around it. It knows that, to use Luther's phrase, sometimes it must "sin bravely," aware that any decision may be greatly enmeshed in sin and ambiguity; but if decisions are to be made, they must be undertaken now, with all the light and love at hand, in reliance upon God's forgiveness for whatever needs forgiveness.

## Dare We Take the Risk?

A major element of significant decision is risk. To many congregations the very mention of risk means financial risk, particularly when the congregation is saddled with a heavy debt. It is hard to be decisive about anything new when a millstone of financial obligations hangs heavy around the congregation's neck. Yet there could hardly be a situation which more compellingly calls for clear decisions involving the fundamental mission of the church. Indifference at this point can only result in decay or insignificance. Any local congregation deep in debt can analyze its debt in the light of its mission.

In 1929 a Tennessee church had its first service in a beautiful new sanctuary. The building was lovely and the debt was massive. As one college professor put it, "Our church is all dressed up but does not know where to go." Ten years later, with the debt still hanging heavy, a new minister moved into the church convinced that above all the congregation needed a new sense of mission. Somehow it had to look beyond itself to the community and the world.

This minister dreamed that the congregation would some day risk itself financially to take responsibility for the support of a missionary overseas. His preaching centered around three themes: (1) strengthen the ministry of the church itself with emphasis on the ministry of the laity, (2) minister to the spiritual and social needs of the immediate community, and (3) extend the ministry overseas by the support of a missionary. The break he had been looking for came in 1944. The Methodist Church embarked on The Crusade for Christ across the nation, and this local church was asked for $11,000. Very easily this congregation could have resented and rejected this goal as another superimposed tax from above. However, the congregation agreed to give, but it wanted its money to go to the support of an overseas missionary. They were told that this was not possible since the Crusade was for general funds not to be specifically so designated. But the church was also told that "anything over and above the amount asked for the Crusade would apply on the support of a missionary." The church was challenged to risk a large sum in the Crusade and risk even more for its dream of an overseas ministry.

A dinner was held for official board members, church school teachers, and officers of other church organizations. The specter of the debt was still there, but also there was a growing vision of a new participation in mission. On the spot those present pledged to the Crusade. They added the pledges up, and to their surprise they found that they alone had subscribed more than had been asked of the entire congregation for the Crusade. The congregation as a whole had not yet been approached! The church was on its way towards support of a missionary in China! Many other pledges came, a sense of mission developed, the missionary they now supported visited their church. A Long-range Planning Committee was created. Three years later a missionary couple in Japan was proposed and added to their growing circle of concern.

About that time came an anonymous gift with an attached note: "This is to be used solely for the support of a missionary, or a missionary couple, to Japan, Korea, or China, whichever the church deems best. This missionary is to be in addition to the present one and the one recently proposed. This is for number three. This amount will be forthcoming yearly for five years." Thus a couple went to Korea.

A year later the church took on support of a minister in Poland. This story continues on. Out of the local church membership came two missionary couples, now serving overseas. The congregation developed interests in Africa and India. Locally a renewed sense of mission has led to all kinds of participation in community projects and organizations that the church considers important. The church grew in membership, effective ministry, and church plant. The terrible old debt was long since retired. A church leader was asked what event in the life of the congregation put the church on the road to greater achievement. His reply was: "When we decided to support a missionary on our own." A decision in the right direction, with real risk, made all the difference.

An area of the congregation's life about which we talk much but often do little, and which entails both risk and opportunity, is the area of local ecumenical relations. As long as ecumenicity is something church leaders discuss in Rome or Geneva or in high-level conferences about interdenominational union, the local congregation can largely pass these discussions by as not germane to its basic life.

It generally does so even when "ecumaniacs" insist that the only forum for genuine ecumenicity is "at the grass-roots" of church life, namely, the local congregation. It is precisely at the level of day in and day out congregational life that there is most risk involved in closer working relationships with a neighbor church or in the eventual organic union of two or more churches in a particular town or city. Ecumenicity taken seriously at this level almost inevitably means entirely new relationships for the pastor, the official bodies that direct the congregation's life, patterns of worship, and channels of activity. It is no wonder that we tend to be reluctant in this field. The risk of change is great.

What makes the risk worth taking is that it almost invariably leads to an experience of enlarged opportunity and of great joy. Beyond that, it lends concretion and embodiment to the reality of one witness in one place in the name of one gospel.

In Schellsburg, Pennsylvania, four "dying churches" representing the United Presbyterian Church in the U.S.A., the Lutheran Church in America, The Methodist Church, and the United Church of Christ existed side by side in a town that had dwindled in population to 288. In April, 1961, a "trial union" was agreed upon, following many discussions of such a plan that went through many stormy seas. It was agreed that the United Church of Christ would appoint a resident pastor while the other three denominations would withdraw any pastoral arrangements they had. This was done in early 1964. In October of that year a new vote on the union was taken with 101 voting in favor, 25 against, and 2 abstaining. Attendance and financial support of the united congregation considerably exceeded the previous combined totals of the four individual congregations. Attendance several times has passed 200 in a town of 288. Worship services have been worked out, using contributions from all four traditions. Above all, the unity of Christ's church has been made crystal clear to everyone in a local situation which cried out for such unity. Renewal sprang from unity which came about at genuine risk.

Risk may ultimately mean some kind of death. In the Schellsburg situation it meant death for three denominations' churches in that place. It meant death for three pastoral appointments, with corresponding salaries and responsibilities. I presume it meant death of some stoutly held committee chairmanships on the various committees of the former four congregations. It surely must have meant that whereas there were once four church treasurers, now only one survived! Certain traditions had to be given up, or modified. Some people have to walk further to church than they did previously. But in spite of all this, and doubtless much more, conscious intentional decision was taken to move towards union. To my mind, this is a good example of what it means to "take up a cross" to follow our Lord. It is a good example of what it means to accept intentionally the meaning of one's own death.

A Christian may not know just when he will die physically. He can know that every day of every year he may die at the points of his existence where it is worth dying for the sake of new life. He knows that renewal springs from repentance. He will allow himself to be caught dead only at the points of significant issues and his own intentional decision.

## THE QUEST FOR NEW STRUCTURES OF OBEDIENCE

The church is "a people claimed by God for his own" for the purpose of mission, "to proclaim the triumphs of him who has called you out of darkness into his marvellous light" (I Peter 2:9). To achieve this end some structure, some channel of work, is necessary and inevitable. Some may want to seek entirely new structures, feeling that present ones are totally inadequate. We maintain that many, if not all, present structures can be renewed to serve acceptably as instruments in this mission.

At what point does a congregation, concerned about renewal and new life, initiate its movement into change? The diversity of ways in which so many congregational groups have gone about this is almost bewildering, so that no one right way emerges.

The point at which some congregations have commenced a penetration of the question is the point of depth Biblical and theological study. Since 1917 when Karl Barth published his epochal *Commentary on Romans,* the theological world has known a ferment and a renewal of gigantic proportions. With it has come a heightened sense of the importance of the Word of God, which has brought a renewed dependence upon Scripture. The Biblical and theological research and discovery of the past generation continues. The results of this massive study are available to any congregation that desires to appropriate them. More than one small group has set out to read a treatise by Barth, Niebuhr, Tillich, Bultmann, or Bonhoeffer and has found itself pressed into searching analysis of its faith and has experienced a new rush of understanding. The theological renewal of recent decades is ours for the taking, and with it comes a renewal of Biblical study and appreciation.

Nevertheless, there is a growing consensus in this day that, important as Biblical and theological study are, it is all too easy for a congregation to stop at the point of this study and fail to implement in the life of the congregation the very ideas which are a product of the theological renewal. The alternative to serious Biblical and theological study is not pure activism devoid of a theological base (such as European churchmen frequently criticize, often rightly, in American churchmen) but rather an infusion into congregational life of some of the major discoveries and insights of theological study. Concurrently with this there must be an awareness of what is going on in the world which has profound bearing upon any understanding of mission. Both the Word and the world set the agenda for the church.

A preliminary document produced in Europe, after expressing concern that the church is on the way to becoming an island separated from the mainland of the new universal society that is arising in an urban-technological age, states that we see emerging "a desire to seek those new structures of Christian life and obedience which will enable the church to witness to the presence of Christ at the place where the fabric of society is at present being woven. We are therefore entering into a second phase of the church's experience of renewal—the move from theological renewal to the quest for new structures of obedience."

The quest for new structures of obedience is the task for which we are claimed. It is the task of every layman and minister as he sets out on a new day of witnessing life. Joseph Mathews has a graphic illustration by which he portrays a congregation as it moves into obedience of this kind. When in New York City at night, he walks through Times Square and looks down through the sidewalk grilles into the blackness which, in pedestrian fact, are the caverns of the New York subway. But he lets his imagination run and conceives that down there somewhere, in those modern catacombs, little groups of Christians are gathered for worship, for study, for scheming and planning their next day's assault upon the world they will face. There they gain mutual strength and courage; there they worship the Lord together; there they plot out their strategy. As dawn comes they quietly disperse, coming up out of the darkness to a new day of light. Now these Christian saints are dressed in gray flannel suits, or in overalls, or in a nurse's uniform, or in a housewife's apron, or in any one of the myriad dresses for the day's tasks, and they scurry off to their appointed places of service. They are still the church of the Lord Jesus Christ, now scattered, weaving into the fabric of that day's life every thread of strategy and witnessing service they have planned the night before. At night they will gather again for an assessment of the day's victories and failures, for a renewed vision of possibility, for a deeper understanding of mission; but always this gathering has only one point of fulfillment, which is in the next day's service, scattered out at the thousand and one points of their existence and concern.

The local congregation is a source of hope because it can discover the centrality of mission to its life, as many congregations today are doing, and can equip laymen for a comprehensive, open, and decisive witness. This is no small order. Old routines cannot hope to match it. Renewed and renewing structures of obedience within the congregation, responsive to God's action in history in our world, are both possible and present. Whether we seek them out, or simply coast along in the placid serenity that nothing need be changed, is our decision.

\* \* \*

### Questions for Discussion

1. Do you agree that most present congregational structures are renewable? Why?
2. What does it mean for your congregation to be comprehensive?
3. If you were to state five major questions that a Christian congregation should continually ask itself as regards its future role, what would they be?
4. Can you give specific examples of decisions taken by your congregation that have involved some measure of risk for the congregation?
5. What does it mean for you and for your congregation to affirm the meaning of your own death? Is this related to repentance?
6. Can you list new "structures of obedience" you would like to see developed in your local congregation?

## chapter III

## CLAIMED BY GOD IN HISTORY

*The development of relevant, renewed structures hinges upon our under-standing of what God is doing in the history he created, in which he re-veals himself, and which he promises to fulfill. A congregation's decision to participate in history forces it to ask the question: what is God doing in history?*

A BABY IS BORN in Montana. A bomb explodes in Vietnam. A neighborhood committee meets in South Carolina. A statesman fashions a new law in Italy. A young man learns to read in Peru. A girl dances in the streets of a nation newly free. All this is part of the welter of present-day history. At any given moment the entire human race has just moved out of an irretrievable past and lives on the knife-edge of the present which itself is fleeting as new presents come to birth out of the future. We see this as the ever-moving flow of history: dynamic, restless, unceasing.

Out of this massive and constant "going-on-ness" we begin to iso-late what appears to have meaning for us. The baby in Montana may appear to be very remote and insignificant to me unless I happen to live in Montana and his mother is my wife. The Vietnam bomb is sorted out from the world of news and spread across the front page because our national future may depend on the next step we take as a nation in that distant land. The South Carolina neigh-borhood committee meeting may seem insignificant until a pro-posal emerges to clear out a slum formerly accepted as necessary.

## GOD ACTS IN HISTORY

In one sense we can say that history is simply the cumulative total of everything that happens. This is not a very helpful concept. No historian expects to capture in his pages everything that happens. Out of this vast mass of occurrences at any moment even the most comprehensive historian is forced to isolate a relatively minute number. He selects those of particular significance. They in themselves may be much like other rejected happenings, but these are peculiar, special, meaningful. They are events. An occurrence plus meaning becomes an event.

It is not altogether unusual for a man to nail a piece of paper to a door; but when Martin Luther nails his theses to a church door, his act has significance far surpassing the moment. It contains in embryo a whole new reformation of the church.

Since the advent of the airplane men have dropped many types of bombs on each other from great heights; but when in 1945 one particular bomb was dropped over Hiroshima, the world knew that an event most ominous for all humanity had taken place.

It is our contention, however, that a Christian congregation does not really have the option of ignoring history so easily. That is to say, if a congregation is to be something more significant than an innocuous group shoring up each other's good feelings, it must have an aim, a purpose reaching out beyond the group itself. It must be related to what is occurring in the world around it. In a word, the church must see that Christian mission involves a relationship in history, and therefore it must take history with the utmost seriousness.

Ultimately this necessity is rooted in the character of God himself. Merely to list a few statements about the God of the Bible is to see that history has tremendous significance for him. What is so important to God must have great importance for any congregation that gathers in his name and endeavors to worship him.

1. *God creates history.* Too easily we imagine that the creation story refers to the birth out of nothing of a static kind of natural

world. There was no earth, but solid earth appeared out of the void, and it was just there. There was no sky, but suddenly there was a sky with a sun and moon and stars in it. There were no fish and animals and people around, but suddenly they appeared, and that is the way it has been ever since. This is the picture of a static universe: God did something once and for all, and it was done. Such a concept misses entirely the meaning of the dramatic creation stories of Genesis. They point symbolically to the initiation of a process in which from the first God participates actively. Indeed, he is the main actor in the drama.

The Biblical creation story was never meant to provide a demonstrable account of the way in which our natural world came into existence. If so, we must admit that it failed. Any grade-school child knows that today's scientists have accumulated evidence that aeons of slow development have gradually brought our natural world to its present state of existence. Only the most naive can equate the complex and scarcely comprehensible stages of this evolution with the first six days of the first chapter of Genesis. The creation story indicates a birth of history, not to be pinpointed in any spot in time or space. God is the author of history, the initiator of the process, the main participant in it. He not only gets history on its way, but he is in the middle of it. He makes it possible though he does not determine everything that happens in it. The only place in which he becomes known to man is as man encounters him in history, either as a God who walks in the cool of the garden or rides the subways of Chicago.

A congregation that takes the God of the Bible seriously takes history seriously as well.

2. *God reveals himself in history.* The only source of our knowledge of God is what God himself opens up to us in the midst of the history he has created. He is seen for what he is in historical events in which he moves, sometimes powerfully, often silently.

A man impelled by God moves out of Ur towards a promised

land, and a new nation is born, chosen in the dawn of our era to bear a special responsibility of witness and obedience. This same people moves out of Egypt in the event of the Exodus, and God's participation in their destiny is felt in deliverance and freedom. In subsequent years he appears as a God of law who does not grant freedom without order. In the ambiguities of national life he appears as a God of justice who will not tolerate privilege that forgets the widow and the poor. In Israel's historical captivity he appears as both sovereign and as suffering, using even his enemies' wrath for the working out of his purposes.

Supremely he makes visible his involvement in history in his incarnation in Jesus Christ. In him we see God's glory, his unbounded love, his identification with our history to the point of becoming a victim of man's sin.

In history God raises up a tiny community of followers who, incredibly, challenge the major empire of the day and become victorious over it. In this historical process God reveals himself as sustaining Spirit, inspiring Word, close participant in the spread of Christianity against seemingly insurmountable odds. In subsequent centuries he is known to men once and again as a God of new life who ever calls men to the deepest meaning of their being and repeatedly works with Christian churches to bring them to a renewed sense of their mission, whether through Augustine, Francis of Assisi, Luther, Wesley, or Kagawa.

This same God reveals himself for those who open their eyes to see him in the squalor of Calcutta, the university campus of Dallas, the industrial complex of Hamburg, and the struggle towards freedom in what remains of colonial Africa. A congregation that takes the God of the Bible seriously searches for God in the history of its own time; and as it meets him in that history, it comes to know what he is like.

3. *God fulfills history.* This may be a bit hard for many of us to accept. There is no question that the Bible record promises a

fulfillment. All things will be gathered up in Christ. The end towards which all moves is an end over which God has dominion even as he was sovereign over the beginning of history. The meaning of the end is intimately tied up with God's purposes for it.

The Biblical record makes no provision for history simply to peter out into meaninglessness or to be blown sky-high by a multimegaton cobalt inferno that ends it all. Even in the not impossible event that this latter disaster might occur, the Biblical faith is that history is not destroyed by man's demonic inventions but, on the contrary, will somehow be completed in God's own good way and time.

Just as we can speak only symbolically of the creation of history, we can speak only symbolically of the end of history. The *end* means not only a terminus in time but a purpose. The end of my life is not solely the moment of my death; it is also, as one confession puts it, "to glorify God and enjoy him forever."

History moves purposively, so we believe, even though daily occurrences confront us with what appears to be total chaos. If a congregation is able to come to some understanding of what God is aiming at through the present processes of history, it can begin to ask itself the fundamental question of how it may participate with God in his mission in history.

## Taking History Seriously

For a congregation to take history seriously it has to adopt a particular stance towards history. Seldom if ever does a congregation do this deliberately. It is a bit difficult to conceive of a congregational meeting at which men and women sit down and ask, "What is our stance this evening towards history?" Nevertheless, the fact is that every congregation implicitly does adopt a stance towards the history in the midst of which it finds itself; hence, it is well to identify what this stance is. Only as it is seen clearly can it be dealt with effectively. What are some attitudes towards history that might be adopted?

1. One is *the attitude that the congregation has nothing to do with history as such.* The realm of religion is concerned with the personal relationship of each individual with God. The church exists to help every individual in it, or outside it, to come to a personal "decision for Christ" in order that he or she may obtain individual salvation and eventually go to the heaven God has promised those who believe in him. This is a complete rejection of the historical process which God has created. God is not to be met in the ambiguities of that process but is "found" in an individual personal relationship (usually, though not necessarily, in a church building or a church activity) which involves personal repentance, forgiveness, restitution, and acceptance of a new life in Christ. In a real sense the individual is saved "out of history." This is not unlike some Oriental religious attitudes that see no meaning in the historical process as such and consequently counsel the religious man to aim at being caught up mystically with the gods who are not subjected to historical vagaries and with whom one's soul is united for perpetual bliss.

According to this attitude, history is concerned primarily with the public realm, while religion has to do with the private realm. Thus history is the realm of national and international affairs, the arena of government on whatever level, the concern of business and commerce, industry and science, the place of hardheaded decisions that must be hammered out. It covers the whole sweep of matters that undoubtedly impinge mightily on individuals as such, but which are the outcome of collective forces over which specific individuals have little to say. By contrast, the religious realm is thought of as the more intimate realm of personal decision, of family life, of right and wrong attitudes, of witness to one's neighbor or his fellow office worker, of prayer and church attendance. This view ascribes politics and business to the secular

60

realm; family and moral decision and worship belong to the religious realm. The former is public and deals with history as we generally conceive it; the latter is private and deals with my relationship to God.

In contemporary American Protestantism the consequence of indifference to history is most clearly seen in the divorce already mentioned between the residential church and the arena of man's daily work. The symbol of this separation is the suburban commuter. He lives in a bedroom community where he sleeps under the same roof as his family, but five mornings a week he kisses them all goodbye and commutes into the place of his work, usually the big city, where he carries on his business. There he decides, he buys and sells, he plans, he earns, he participates in public life, he makes his contribution to society. Back home mother struggles through the day trying to keep a semblance of order with the children, cleaning the perennially dirty house, chit-chatting with the neighbors, and preparing a meal for her exhausted husband to eat that evening when he returns from work to rest. At which end of the commuter's trip is the church? Almost invariably at the home end, away from the forum of the man's work and decision. It is present near man's residence to provide weekend inspiration, Christian education for children and youth, and a pastor for visitation of the sick and comfort of the bereaved.

The point is that this residential church is stoutly defended by many as the only proper order of things, in complete consonance with the attitude that religion has nothing to do with the public realm—the whole process of history—and that the Christian congregation's concern should necessarily be limited to a religious realm that is essentially private and personal.

2. Another stance towards history that a congregation might adopt is *to assume that the direction of history is predetermined* and that there is no point in challenging it or attempting to deter it. This can take many forms. It can mean for some people a sur-

render to sheer indifference. What happens is bound to happen, so let it happen. For others it may mean a genuine conviction that all is in God's hands, so why worry about what occurs in history? God knows what he is doing. He will not let evil win out in the end. Whatever crises history may face along its way, the outcome is sure, and God will take care of it.

A current concept of this type is the belief in progress. It is not simply an empirical observation that history has given evidence of the expansion of knowledge, the growth of technology, and vast improvements in the physical and environmental conditions of man's life. It is rather the belief that progress is inevitable and that something in the very nature of history and of the universe makes it necessary. As man wrests new secrets from the universe through scientific research, as he develops improved means of communication, as education becomes available to all in ever increasing quantities, as men understand more clearly the motivations by which they act—all this will result in a necessary improvement in the state of mankind. History cannot be reversed, and things are bound to get better. This is the way the world is set up. This inevitability is even transferred from the area of material improvement and scientific knowledge to the area of moral condition, so that presumably we will be both more enlightened and more moral than we now are. Time will take care of this. Progress is basically automatic and predetermined.

Granting the appeal of the theory of inevitable progress which many of our contemporaries choose to believe and many others seem to take for granted, historical determinism is difficult to substantiate, particularly in the moral and spiritual realm. Two world wars in this century, the development of instruments of destruction unimagined in prior centuries, and the diabolical uses of genocide, brainwashing, and mass propaganda are but a few of the facts of our day which weigh heavily against the idea that our capacity for evil is diminishing or that progress inevitably results.

It appears to be possible, for the first time in human history, that this doctrine may have no chance of final vindication if humanity succeeds in its own extinction, an outcome that would itself prove the fallacy of the idea. This is simply to say that this concept is closer to disproof today than it ever was before, though we all hope its propounders will be around a long time to hold it if they wish!

Another version of this view of history is Marxism. For the Marxist the direction of history is predetermined. He is very optimistic about history. He believes nothing can defeat the eventual appearance of a classless society. This will occur whether men and societies oppose it or not. This is just one of the "givens" of life. Our question is simply whether this is a true reading of the nature of history. There is very good reason to assert it is not.

3. A third stance that a congregation may take is *to decide to participate in history* in so far as it can. At first glance such a statement appears foolish, since we are thrown into historical existence without our decision. It is like saying that I will decide to breathe. The comparison, however, is not quite correct. I am an historical being, whether I like it or not. I am in the flux of history, and no rocket can get me out of it. To this extent I am in history until my death. But mentally, internally, I can choose to affirm this fact and actively seek out its implications, or I can presume to deny the meaning of this fact and shun its implications. Either decision does not change the fact that I have been thrown into history and here I am, but which decision I choose makes all the difference in the world concerning my life and my participation in the history around me. The same is true of a congregation.

The two attitudes to history previously presented involve either an implicit or a conscious decision not to affirm history as a meaningful arena for the life and work of a congregation. They reject history either because they see no meaning in it, or feel it is not a proper object of their concern, or because its outcome is predetermined anyway, and thus rob it of importance. They do

63

not take history seriously and consequently see no relation between the history around them and the congregational life of those who gather in the name of Christ. A most serious consequence of this stance, if our prior analysis is correct, is that those who hold such views deliberately reject that which God has created, the arena in which God reveals himself, and that which God fulfills. To do this is to move the church right out of the area God has chosen as the area within which he will act.

## What Is God Doing?

What, then, does it mean for a congregation to decide to participate in history in so far as it can? A great deal, but a primary question it will set before itself and wrestle with in prayer and study is this fundamental question: *What is God doing in our history?* No other question, earnestly asked and carefully answered (however tentative preliminary answers may have to be), has more profound implications for the life of a Christian congregation today and for the structures which a congregation will adopt in living out the implications of its answers.

The question itself contains a number of assumptions. We do well to examine them. First, it assumes that God *is* active in our history. This is not an assumption that all men make, not even all Christians. In recent years, particularly since the publication of Bishop J. A. T. Robinson's much-discussed book, *Honest to God,* an attack has been leveled at any idea of God which would in some way locate him "up there" in some distant heaven or in some intellectual compartment from which he looks "down" on us and on history. It is not just that astronauts have burst out into a space we had never explored hitherto and found that God is not "up there." Nor is it an attempt to deny the transcendence of God with all that this involves in omnipotence and omniscience. It is rather an effort to direct our attention to the one place where God is most readily encountered, yet so often least easily recognized, namely, the history of the world. Instead of our looking "up there" somewhere pleading that he may "send down" some blessing upon us from "on high," we direct our gaze into the historical world of struggle, business, politics, art, family, wars, decisions, budgets, taxes, and all that makes up our history. If we insist on locating God somewhere (this is not necessary, but we seem to have difficulty avoiding it), it may be helpful to picture him "out there" in the middle of a history into which we move to find him at work. The decision to participate in history on the part of a congregation really means that it will assume God is at work in the history around it and that it will try to find out what this work of God is.

In 1962 I was traveling in Chile, about a year after the terrible earthquakes that shook the southern part of that nation and took over five thousand lives, leaving many more persons homeless. I was shown some of the scars of that catastrophe and then was told of the gigantic effort the government was making to provide homes for the many families who had lost their previous residences. I was told that in the year since the earthquake already some 100,000 new houses, most of them simple yet adequate, had been built for these families, so that at that time many of the beneficiaries of this building program had homes that were far better than some of the miserable shacks they had once occupied. Almost instinctively I said, "Thank God!" The man next to me quickly said, "Don't thank God, thank the government that built them!" I was grateful that the government had done what it had, but it seemed to me justifiable to assume that in some way God was active in the history of Chile during that year in the provision of adequate housing for 100,000 families. At least it seemed intolerable to me to assume the opposite, namely, that God had nothing at all to do with the provision of such housing, that he did not care whether those families were properly housed or not and that this whole thing was a purely governmental task unrelated to anything God does in history.

I am well aware that to raise the question in this way immediately poses a wealth of other questions, foremost among them the query as to what criteria we can use to determine what is and what is not God's work. If God is at work in history, and if not everything that occurs in history is of God's direct doing (as I think we can safely assume, since otherwise we would make God responsible for all that is sinful, destructive, dishonest, and degrading), then it is fair to ask for some criterion by which to know what is God's work and what is not. The immediate temptation is to set up a list of such criteria. Some congregations may find such an attempt helpful. The caution one would raise at such a procedure is that whatever criteria are listed must be seen as a preliminary and tentative list, always subject to review, because of our inability to discern with any final certainty the mysteries of God's activity. This is another way of saying that any judgments we make about what is or what is not God's activity must be held in humility.

Never dare we be too sure that God's activity is plain to see lest we fall into the insufferable pride of presuming to know what God knows and claiming such knowledge as a justification for our very human endeavors that we too easily equate with God's activity. But the question of what God is doing in our history must be asked. Preliminary answers must be given.

An initial supposition that may help us to see what God is doing is to assume that his present work in history is in harmony with his eternal purposes disclosed to us in the Bible. The more we can fathom and understand the great acts of God in creation, election of a people, prophetic witness, incarnation, creation of the Christian church, and promise of eventual fulfillment, the more prepared we are to look at our twentieth-century world and discern, with eyes of faith, what God appears to be doing now.

A second assumption behind the question "What is God doing in our history?" is that our mission can best be known when we know what God is doing in his mission. We may think we know what our mission is, and we may pursue it assiduously; but conceivably, even though it does some good, it might be contrary to God's major purposes in a given historical situation.

I was told of a discussion that took place in Rhodesia, one of the African nations that has not at this writing received its independence from colonial status. Christians were discussing the future and frankly faced the possibility that if the independence movements gained strength, violence against white men might break out. What then is the mission of the church in the midst of such a situation? One Christian leader stood up and made a statement to this effect: "When chaos comes, I fear Christians will too easily focus their attention on the wrong issue, namely violence. You will want to do everything possible to avoid violence to anyone, and that is understandable. But if a man is sitting on top of your head, even if you wiggle your ears that is violence to the man up there. The real issue is to get the man off your head. The real issue in Rhodesia is the transfer of power from the colonial power to the black African Rhodesians, who constitute by far the largest population group in the country." Is this not another way of saying that the mission could appear to be the elimination or avoidance of violence (a laudable aim) when God is at work in the liberation of a whole nation, helping it to secure its own destiny with power in the hands of the governed? In any case, our mission must be related to what God is doing. How potentially dangerous this can be!

One of the most difficult problems with which mission board administrators grapple is the future of some of the large institutions Christian missionaries have helped develop in many nations around the world. Fine schools have been erected, staffed, and maintained, some of them with ample support in personnel and funds from the West. The same can be said about hospitals, social centers, agricultural demonstration centers, and others. Every institution is a monument to the concern of one or more persons who, supported by thousands of others, saw it as part of their mission to help create such an institution. The massive testimony these Christian institutions around the world provide to the Christian concern of dedicated men and women is most impressive. We can be grateful for the significant contribution these institutions have made in terms of education, healing, training national leadership, improving farming methods, and a vast number of other services. Today, however, we must ask ourselves what our mission is, given the realities of this day, which are far different from what they were fifty or a hundred years ago.

In some of these countries public education, for example, has made great strides, so that mission schools are no longer providing the only good education, or even the best academic training. Furthermore the demands of these institutions have increased. They require funds which the local churches of these countries often cannot hope to provide. Their needs for teachers are so evident that they easily take precedence over personnel for extremely important tasks, such as evangelism in newly industrialized areas, for few are clamoring for such evangelists. Church resources get immobilized in institutions which sometimes provide a questionable, or at best a minimal, Christian witness.

The question that plagues more than one mission board administrator and local advisory committee is this: What is our mission today with regard to an institution that appears to have slipped from a place of central importance? Shall funds and personnel no longer be sent to support the institution, with all the agony that may mean? Shall more funds and personnel be provided to attempt to raise the standards of the institution to make it the very best it can be and to strengthen greatly its Christian witness in the community? And is this to be done if it means denying personnel and funds to other more needy and equally worthy projects or institutions? What if God's activity in education in that nation appears to

68

be centered now at some other point, such as teacher training to provide able teachers for a growing public school system, or university education for a new professional class that will soon hold the destiny of the nation in its hand? How does the church readjust to such a situation?

A local congregation faces similarly difficult problems. This fact becomes painfully evident for congregations that are located in changing neighborhoods. Once the building served those who resided nearby. Now with few exceptions all have moved away. The church is now surrounded by Spanish-speaking Latins from Puerto Rico, Cuba, and Mexico. What is its mission now? Is it to pull up stakes and follow some of its former families into suburbia, as so many churches have done with every good intention of providing religious services to their members? Note, however, the difference between a church as mission and an institution that provides services for its members only! Or is the congregation to seek seriously for what God is doing in that changing neighborhood, a search which may cast a whole new light both on the plans to move and on the nature of the mission of that congregation?

### HE IS ACTIVE INSIDE AND OUTSIDE THE CHURCH

A third assumption behind the question, "What is God doing in our history?" is that God is active both inside and outside the church. The equation of God's sphere of activity with the church is made with the greatest of ease, particularly by those of us who happen to grow up in a Christian church and associate the church with God's activity almost by second nature. At the very least we have frequently taken it for granted that God works in the world *through* the church. By the "church" we have generally had in mind the congregation which had become institutionalized with a building, a schedule, a pastor, and a program. "God has no other hands but yours, no other feet but yours, no other voice but yours." And "yours" means you of the congregation. So we have thought.

Even a superficial reading of the Biblical record indicates that such a situation was not always the case. It is true that God chose a special people for a particular mission at a given time, but he never said to Israel that he would limit his work in the world to what he did to and through Israel. In fact, Israel was well aware of this and knew that God had power to act in other nations and to use their national life for his purposes. The favorite verse of many a Sunday school child, "God so loved the world he gave his only Son . . ." (John 3:16) does not even mention the church. God's love encompasses the entire world, which includes the church but is not limited to it.

This matter is noted in Colin Williams' comments on Professor Casalis' presentation in one of the studies made of the "missionary structure of the congregation" in Europe:

Professor Casalis raised the issue at the first meeting of the Western European Working Group when he said that in the Church we have developed the habit of thinking in the order *God-Church-World,* whereas the Biblical witness should lead us to think the other way around: *God-World-Church.* God is not concerned first with the Church, and we should not think of the Church as God's sole partner, with God and the Church directing their action at the world. God is first concerned with the world (Casalis insists); it is there that he is at work working out *his purpose for the world.* The Church is simply a part of the world— the part which is aware of Christ's Lordship over the world, and so is ready to recognize what God is doing in the world and to join him in that action.[1]

It may not be immediately easy for us to shift our habitual pattern of thinking to conceive of God working primarily out in the world by himself, instead of channelling his activity in the world through the church. Yet we can scarcely come to terms with the Biblical witness or with a realistic observation of all the creative

---

[1] Colin Williams, *Where in the World?,* page 76.

movements at work in the world without concluding that God is highly active in many realms which the church is not touching at all. Thus we are brought back to the demand that we attempt to identify what God is doing in this world in order that as a church we may place ourselves at the points where God is carrying on his mission.

How do we know what God is doing in the world? One can hardly ask a more difficult question. The difficulty is compounded by the great mass of answers that are submitted to this question by students and observers of historical processes. These answers suffer from one major defect, namely, the lack of involvement of the observer in the processes he presumes to describe. Without for a moment disparaging the value of academic analysis and of rigorous thought, we can set down as a fundamental principle the following: God's work in a given area of the world can best be identified and understood by those who immerse themselves in the world they are trying to understand. Another way to put this is to say that our mission begins to come clear to us when we, in sheer faith, step out into uncertain areas of the world's need and simply try to be a Christian presence there. As we do so, what God is doing there begins to appear to those intently desirous of discerning it.

In the foreword I mentioned the book, *The Cross and the Switchblade*. Whatever one may think about the theology of the author, here is a remarkable story about a man who came under the conviction that he was called by God to participate personally in the devastatingly complex world of the New York City teen-age delinquent. As he tells the story, he did not have the slightest idea as to what he might do or how he might go about implementing his conviction. All he knew he must do was to go to New York, be there, and see what developed, confident that God would point out next steps. The fascinating story that ensues is one of a growing sense of mission which came as he became aware of ways in which,

71

to his understanding, God was already at work in the lives and gangs of the teen-agers.

It is certain that I, who have never been deeply involved in the New York world of juvenile delinquency, narcotics addiction, and sheer loneliness, do not have the faintest idea of what God is doing in that world and that any judgments I may make about his activity there are at best second- or third-hand and to that extent of little value. What God is doing in his mission at that point is best seen and understood by the man who risks everything to plunge into that world without any advance preconceptions about what his mission is and begins to sort out, from the multitudinous impressions he receives, some inductive understanding of what God is trying to do.

We cannot really know what our mission is until we get out into it. This statement may seem the height of folly: if we do not know what our mission is, how can we move into it? It would seem we are caught in a vicious circle. We cannot know what our mission is until we move into mission, yet how do we move into it if we do not know what it is? Such an argument, however, fails to take account of the fact that God breaks into the circle and opens up to the Christian a knowledge of what next steps he might take and an insight into what he is doing, *if* the Christian is really open to see with eyes of faith and is eager to know what God is doing. This is not mere optimistic hopefulness, but it is confirmed time and time again by those who have actually done it. The meaning of history and of God's participation in it is unfolded—always tentatively, never fully—to those who risk real participation in it.

In the early days of the East Harlem Protestant Parish one of its leaders referred in conversation to some of the surprises the members of the parish program had received. As in those early days they immersed themselves in the problems and complexities of East Harlem, they found themselves literally driven to seek solutions in forums that they might well have preferred to avoid.

They were wholly convinced that God was leading them into a participation in his history in East Harlem at points they never dreamed of until they were actually there. Thus the battle for even minimally decent housing in the area could not be fought out in the circumscribed area of East Harlem alone. It had to be carried to City Hall, where new and more adequate legislation could be sought; to city administrative units which could be prevailed on to enforce the legislation already on the books and studiously ignored; to the police department, which traditionally saw East Harlem as its "Siberia" for the discipline of errant policemen; and to the doors of suburban landlords who lived off exorbitant rents from East Harlem tenements, but who simply ignored the most elemental responsibilities any landlord has in the maintenance and upkeep of a reasonably safe and livable building.

How could anyone know what God was doing in Eart Harlem, or what he might want to do, unless he placed himself in East Harlem with an inquiring mind of faith to find out? How can any congregation know what God is doing in the history of the world around it until in some way it simply places itself in a position to receive insight for next steps, then takes these steps, and moves to a new position of readiness for a bit more light and a bit more demand upon it?

This does not necessarily mean that such a presence must always be physical. A congregation in Wyoming cannot physically transplant itself to Tunisia to find out what God is doing there and to wait for God's revelation of light as to next steps. It may rely upon the written reports of some missionary in Tunisia, or it may be fortunate enough to have some member of the congregation travel to Tunisia to bring back firsthand information. It may well decide, however, that as a congregation it will select Tunisia as an area of its mission concern and will be "present" to Tunisia's problems and needs by a conscious effort to learn everything it can about Tunisia (which in this day of readily available information and

73

communication immediately becomes a very large task) in order that even at a distance it may share in God's work there. This sharing may well be translated into concrete support of those who, in the name of the Christian gospel, attempt to participate on the ground in God's mission in Tunisia. At least the opposite can be affirmed: the Wyoming congregation will not be able to know what God is attempting to do in Tunisia nor participate intelligently in that mission unless the congregation makes a definite effort to be present to Tunisia in any and every way open to it.

When I first went out as a Methodist missionary to a place in Uruguay called Salto, I wondered far into many nights what God could possibly want me to do there. What was his mission in that city of fifty thousand persons? What was he already doing there? I recall vividly the first day I was in Salto, in 1953, waiting hours on end in a vacant house for the arrival of our trunks and furniture. There was nothing to do but wait and think. After all the earlier decisions about entering missionary service, here suddenly I was at the place of my mission; and I had to admit that I did not have the faintest idea either of what God was doing in Salto already or of what he expected me to do. I spent that day with a pocket New Testament trying to fathom out what my mission might be. When the day ended, the trunks and furniture had not come; and neither was I any further along in an understanding of my mission in Salto, or of God's. It was only as in time I began to walk through the streets of that city, visit in the homes of neighbors, share in the lives and faith of a few already there whose Christian convictions and faith made mine look weak that slowly I began to sense what God might be aiming at in that community—only then did the wealth of mission opportunity come to life in my own mind. And only then did the New Testament promises and demands speak forth their vivid meaning for me.

One example of the way in which it seemed God opened up channels of understanding and service came as we struggled with the problem of where we as a congregation would meet. In nine years we roamed around from one rented house to another—six in all—to a point where the community began to wonder where the Methodist church would be meeting next! If mobility is a mark of a Christian congregation, we were on the right track! Early in this process an elderly rough-hewn saint (in the Corinthian sense) marched into a Sunday evening service with a cookie tin under his arm, dropped a few pennies into it, and announced to anyone who cared to listen that he had just initiated a fund for the eventual purchase of a piece of land the congregation might call its own. On this land the new Salto Methodist Church would be built. Some of us smiled politely and dared not think how long it would take for those pennies to multiply in order that this gentleman's dream might be realized. But he had put us on the way. He plunged into an area of mission he felt was important. Next steps would be for all of us together to find.

Four years later, when the contents of that cookie-tin fund were still pitifully small by comparison with what was needed, I was asked to visit a lady who wished to talk with me. Before that conversation was over she had turned over to this struggling new congregation a gift of a property worth at that time about $20,000! She felt this congregation, as it attempted to know something of God's will in Salto's history, might well be ready to participate constructively in God's mission there in a new and expanded way. Almost speechless with emotion, I could not put into words my own feelings at that point. I could not help recalling the old gentleman and the cookie tin. Without his venture into mission as he saw it, I felt sure no one, least of all this lady, would have seen any reason to add to the content and meaning of that tin.

The point of this story is as old as Christianity itself: new understanding of God's mission and, consequently, of our mission in history comes most readily to the individual or the congregation that gets into mission with no guarantees of success and the high risk of total failure. To find mission the congregation must be in mission. To know what God is doing in our history, there is no short cut around a willing dive into the history into which God, whether we like it or not, has already thrown us.

* * *

## Questions for Discussion

1. Is it possible for us to know what God is doing in our history?
2. Does the astounding development of modern science and technology reinforce a belief in inevitable progress? Is such inevitable progress part of the moral realm?
3. How would your congregation decide to "participate in history"?
4. List the five major signs you can see of God's activity in the history of today's world.
5. To what extent must we know what God is doing in history before we can know our own mission?
6. Does suburban congregational life tend to remove many congregations from significant participation in today's history? How?

## chapter IV

---

# THE NEW WORLD AT OUR DOOR

*Relevant structures for the congregation in our twentieth-century world must be responsive to what God is now doing in our shifting, surging, secularized, suffering, and searching world.*

O NE OF the phrases that has emerged in the study of "the missionary structure of the congregation" is this: *the world sets the agenda for the church.* What does this mean? Negatively it means that the church cannot know what its mission is in isolation from the world around it. The mission of the church is not to be found inside the church building or within the fellowship of the congregation. On the contrary, what goes on inside the congregation, as it gathers for worship and study, is merely a preparation for dealing with the agenda which the surrounding world imposes upon the church. If the congregation is to know what it must be and do, it will have to look beyond itself. The structures of the world's needs will largely determine the task of the congregation and hence the structures through which the congregation will work.

A local congregation in Milford, Connecticut faced this very problem. Laymen of the church wrestled long and hard with their own responsibility as a congregation and came to the statement that "the nature of the community we have to serve will determine to a large extent the kind of mission that will be relevant." At the same time they confessed that they were "unready for such adventures." Presumably most of these men and women thought they knew their community fairly well until they probed more deeply into the needs of the community, the hidden and silent needs, the evidence of family disarray, political power, delinquency, racial problems, community resources, and so on. They wrote: "We confess with concern that we do not know where to start. . . . The reason for our ignorance is that we have not taken either our mission or our world seriously for a long time." [1]

Such forthright honesty and candor are refreshing. In too many church circles there is neither a sense of ignorance nor a concern to delve systematically into a study of the nature of the world surrounding us. The minute a congregation in effect "turns itself outward" to seek a realistic understanding of the community beyond its doors, and does so deliberately with the purpose of endeavoring to see what the community picture says to the congregation, there is great hope.

We may not know what a congregation must do to relate itself creatively to the whole stream of human history, but it can look at Milford, or a St. Louis neighborhood, or a Portland community and begin to isolate what seem to be some of the major community problems and needs. The focus of the church's attention is then beyond itself.

The "world" of which we speak is to be seen both theologically and sociologically. On the one hand, theologically, it is the arena of God's activity in history. We take this world seriously because God takes it seriously. If God has chosen it for his work place, we have to do the same. As a congregation turns itself outward to the world, it does so with the constant question in mind, "What is God doing here in this world?" On the other hand, sociologically, the world is the arena of historical occurrences involving people and their daily relationships, with the myriad groupings that men and women devise or fall into. Here we see the world as people impinging upon

---

[1] Mimeographed Report of Winter Seminar, January-February 1964, Church of Christ, Congregational, Milford, Connecticut.

one another, weaving fabrics of interrelationship, fighting or loving, at work or at leisure, leading or being led, concerned or indifferent.

The congregation deals with both views of the world and may have some difficulty in separating one from another. The attempt to understand the surrounding community involves gathering data and isolating major problems. This in itself is a more formidable task than most congregations choose to undertake. As they do so, they will begin to reflect on the data they gather from the vantage point of faith. All the resources of Biblical study, worship, church history, and doctrinal analysis provide insights to help answer the question, "What is God doing in this community?"

The purpose of this chapter is to point to five major movements in our contemporary world which are relevant to the life of the church as a whole and which any congregation will have to take into account as it searches for its mission in today's world. We speak here in broad terms of global movements, but no one of these is far from the doorstep of any local congregation. All impinge upon the life of every individual of the twentieth century and are part of the history which we must affirm and within which we have to seek our role as Christian congregations.

## A Shifting World

The most apparent and arresting fact of our age is the fact of rapid change. Any analysis of the society around us, whether it be of the entire geographical world or of the closest knit small community, must commence with the recognition of the fact of astounding change, which alters the nature and meaning of human relationships. To be sure, the fact of change in itself is not new. No period of time and no communal grouping has ever been impervious to change. The startling reality of the twentieth century is the rapidity of change. Suddenly we are aware as never before of the sweeping nature of change which is almost breathtaking. What we considered certain and stable yesterday has disappeared by today, and today's foundations will almost surely be shaken by tomorrow.

As Dow Kirkpatrick stated in an address in Washington, D.C., in 1963: "Change is a fact. This must be the first and unmistakably clear declaration of any missionary message. Change is a fact. But, you say, nobody needs to go about preaching that. Everyone does not know it. Everyone has heard about it, but not everyone knows it. Not everyone accepts it as that which must be accepted."

Norman Cousins, in an editorial graphically entitled "Life Inside the Centrifuge" put it this way:

Into a few decades have been compressed more change, more thrust, more tossing about of men's souls and gizzards, than had been spaced out over most of the human chronicle until then. The entire metabolism of history has gone berserk.[2]

To comprehend this rapid change we point to examples. The American Bible Society has a new machine which among its many talents can print up the addresses of all who are to receive *Bible Society Record,* the society's monthly journal. Approximately a million copies are sent out monthly. It has been estimated that one typist working full time would require several years of work to type up all the addresses required for a single month's issue. But now automation is present, and this machine can do the same job in a couple of hours. A few buttons are pushed, and then, independently of any human effort, the million addresses are poured out. Computers, memory banks, and every variety of data-processing machines suddenly make available to us virtually instantaneous calculations and complex analyses of which only a few short years ago man dared not even dream.

Change is fostered and stimulated by the scientific revolution of our time. There are more scientists alive today than the total number

[2] *Saturday Review,* August 29, 1964, page 60.

of all the scientists of all ages of man put together prior to 1920. The presence in the world of such a body of men, relentlessly searching out the secrets of matter and nature, is an entirely new phenomenon with which our grandparents did not have to deal. The combination of massive research with an immense and growing technological capacity to produce goods and services confronts every man and every society with an upheaval in patterns of consumption, living, and relationship.

Change affects our very concept of time—as someone has said, "A year is not a year anymore." Change not only impinges upon the material aspects of our lives but slashes into our psychological patterns and spiritual bastions. Its implications can scarcely be estimated. To quote Norman Cousins again:

In the centrifuge of the twentieth century, man is whirling away from the center of his own being. The farther out he spins, the more blurred his view of himself, of what he might be, and of his relationship to the nameless faces in the crowd. The separation is not just between the body and place; it is between mind and reason. Ultimately the acceleration produces irreverence.[3]

This last statement alone is food for thought for any congregation. If as Christians we have seen ourselves as dealing with "eternal verities" or "stable moral values" or "abiding principles," we do well to face squarely the fact that the onrush of revolutionary change in our day tends in itself to withdraw men from even the most meager consideration of stable factors which may have seemed significant to Christians. It is as though the spin of events is so fast and dizzying that all efforts must be bent to hang on, with no time or disposition left to consider what makes everything spin or what ultimate meanings may be affirmed or challenged in the process.

Four aspects of this rapid change are particularly significant for a congregation. The first is that the world is rapidly becoming a differ-

---

[3] *Ibid.*

ent place from what it was in the relatively recent past due to *the tremendous increase in population.* If we think of the world as people, rather than as a geographical place, it is a speedily growing world.

Figures and statistics on the world's population explosion tend to overwhelm us, yet they cannot be dismissed. A recent bulletin was entitled, "1964 World Population: 3.3 Billion—Another Billion Expected by 1980." [4] It points out that annually the world population is growing by approximately 65 million people, "enough to populate a new nation larger than West Germany or the United Kingdom." Another way to picture this astounding development is to recognize that enough people are added to the population of the world every month to add a city of Chicago, or every two weeks to add a city of Detroit. Since from 80 to 100 individuals are added to the world's population every minute, at every beat of your pulse the world has at least one additional mouth to feed!

More than half the world's people live in Asia. The United States, the Soviet Union, and Europe account for roughly only one quarter of the population. The high birthrate countries are almost uniformly those with lower levels of material living. The most populous country in the world is China. One out of every four or five births today is Chinese. India, the world's second largest nation, gains approximately ten million new people each year, more than the total population of Sweden.

The most rapid growth rate is in Latin America. Every ten seconds a child is born in Brazil. Brazil can be expected to double its population in 23 years.

The whole world will double its population in 35 years, which means that by the year 2000 we can look forward to approximately seven billion persons if present growth rates remain constant.

Such figures have formidable implications for any church that

---

[4] Bulletin of Office for Research, Commission on Ecumenical Mission and Relations of The United Presbyterian Church in the U.S.A., Vol. IV, No. 5, December 15, 1964.

senses a worldwide responsibility. They have significance as well
for the mission of the most isolated local congregation. No community is exempt from being engulfed by an influx of unexpected
population.

The fact of population growth points up a whole list of needs.
Paramount among them is the need to control this growth in some
rational manner. Otherwise the grim future is that of growing poverty, hunger, housing deficiency, despair, and intensified violence
almost certainly eventuating in war. The Division of Overseas Ministries of the National Council of Churches has recently taken an
encouraging step in the creation of an office with competent personnel to give full time to the stimulation of family planning overseas
and the dissemination of information that may contribute to a cli-
mate both of concern and of responsibility in this area.

The church may see in these statistics ominous suggestions that its
own percentage of the world's population is decreasing. The growth
of the Christian church is not nearly keeping pace with the world's
population growth. The facts may be interpreted as a call for massive evangelism of vast new proportions. It is surprising to read
that in a day when presumably Christianity has covered the geo-
graphic face of the globe, there are at least ten thousand villages in
Ceylon alone in which the name of Jesus Christ has not even been
heard.[5]

Unquestionably there is a call to mission here for anyone
who senses an urgency that Christ be proclaimed to those who never
once heard of his life or work or love. Such thinking, though valid,
may be corrupted if it simply springs from the church's instinct of
self-preservation. The population explosion poses before the church
a radical problem of escalating human need. It is a need beyond the
church itself to which the church cannot close its eyes. The nature
of the need, which may take on different aspects in different areas, is

---

[5] Webster, *op. cit.*, page 17.

a fundamental concern of the Christian church as it seeks out its mission.

Second, *the world is rapidly shrinking in size,* so that every part of the world is on the doorstep of every congregation. The revolution in communications is so much a part of our daily living that it need not be documented here. The congregation which until recently was related to a limited and manageable number of nearby neighborhoods now finds that what occurs in communities thousands of miles away suddenly becomes urgent business for it. News media relay almost instantly to the congregation the report of incidents that forty years ago would have been too far away to deserve notice. A Congo uprising, an Alabama civil rights march, a Cuban missile base, a Russian satellite launching, a transfer of power in Bolivia, all are immediately within the circle of interest and concern of men everywhere. What my community is and does may well be headline news tomorrow in Thailand. The world is so small that the tragedies and joys of any man are immediately thrust before all of us.

In a very real sense this small world greatly facilitates the task of the man of faith. He and the congregation of which he is a part must know that he cannot overlook the comprehensive nature of his calling. To be parochial, concerned with a small and limited segment of the world to the deliberate exclusion of concern for the totality of the inhabited world, is both anomalous and self-defeating. It is still possible for a congregation to pretend that it lives to itself alone. We can close out the sounds of a world pressing in upon us, but it is increasingly difficult.

The comprehensiveness of faith, encompassing the entire universe, is more credible today than it was only a few short years ago when a congregation gave evidence of its comprehensiveness only by sending funds to support some barely known missionary at work among "the heathen." Today the farthest foreign mission outpost is neither far away nor foreign to any congregation unless the congregation,

84

through sheer indifference or deliberate blindness, blots out of mind what every newspaper and television station proclaims from the housetops.

Third, the world is rapidly becoming *an urbanized world*. The movement of enormous populations into concentrated urban areas began towards the close of the last century. It is now a worldwide phenomenon. Tokyo, Rome, São Paulo, and Los Angeles are but a few of the jammed masses of humanity crowding into close living quarters. In New York City there are areas where as many as two hundred thousand persons live vertically over one square mile. The trends toward increasing concentration across the United States continue.

In 1850, only 15 out of every 100 people [in our nation] lived in a city or other urban area. At the turn of the century, urban areas were home for 40 out of every 100 people. By 1950, 64 percent of the population lived in urban areas, and the proportion has continued to rise. Today almost three-fourths of all Americans live in an urban area. About one-half of them live in the 212 Standard Metropolitan Statistical Areas, that is, in cities of 50,000 or larger and the surrounding county or counties.[6]

What this means in terms of changes in the rank of cities in our country is amusingly evidenced by the following:

The U.S. Census of 1850 revealed that the ninth and eleventh largest cities in the country were Spring Garden and Northern Liberties, Pennsylvania. Long ago these cities were annexed by Philadelphia. The sole vestiges of Spring Garden today are a street name and eleven entries in the Philadelphia telephone book, one of them being Spring Garden Methodist Church, a part of the Fairmont Inner City Parish. Of Northern Liberties there is no trace. In 1960 the ninth and eleventh largest

---

[6] *Horizons in Home Missions*, 1964, prepared by the Department of Research and Survey, National Division, Board of Missions of The Methodist Church, page 9.

cities were Washington, D.C., and San Francisco. Where will they be in the census of 2060? [7]

It is interesting to note two related developments: one is the gradual growth of the "strip city," sometimes called megalopolis, as adjoining metropolitan areas merge into each other. Washington to Boston, San Diego to San Francisco, Milwaukee to Chicago, and Jacksonville to Miami are examples of varying magnitude. The other development closely related to this is the more recent emergence of "fringe cities," which arise as inner-city inhabitants move out of an area of very heavy concentration in search of equally urban but less concentrated centers of population. In the last U.S. census eleven of the twenty largest cities in the United States lost population; but, far from indicating a reversal of the urbanization trend, this fact merely points to the upsurge of new metropolitan areas strung out across the country, often as satellites to the larger demographic centers.

The fact of urbanization is important in view of all the problems a church faces in a city, but equally important for the church is a recognition of what urbanization means in terms of mind-set and attitude. It can truly be said today that every man is an urban man. To be urban is not conditioned on living within a particular city limit. The rural man is today anachronistic and virtually extinct. What is implied in the statement that every man today is urban? First, he desires and accepts the products that are characteristically produced by an urban-technological society. Second, he knows the power is concentrated at urban centers and therefore he concentrates his hopes for physical and social betterment at those centers, whether he lives in them or not. Third, his orientation is essentially collectivistic rather than individualistic. Justice and rights are secured by social groupings that work through channels available mainly at urban centers. Fourth, he knows he is dependent for his welfare and future,

---

[7] *Ibid.*, page 14.

as every city man is, upon a multitude of forces and people, generally unknown to him. Gone is any possible self-sufficiency pictured as part of the good old rural days. Fifth, he is increasingly aware of the unity of mankind, even in spite of political or international divisions. Urban man in Singapore and urban man in Santiago have more in common in their way of life than either one of them has with his rural ancestors of two generations ago.

What does this urban trend say to the Christian congregation? Suffice it at this point to remember that most residential congregations of our day derive their structures and practices from rural settings. The parish evokes a picture of the white-steepled church at the very heart of a rural town at which stalwart farmers and their families gather on placid Sunday mornings for worship and song. This does not quite fit the complexities of downtown Chicago. The itinerant ministry calls up a picture of Bishop Francis Asbury on horseback as he carried the gospel from hamlet to town across the early frontier. It does not quite fit the modern bishop or the minister of a 5000-member church whose operation bears similarity to the high-powered pressures of a corporation executive. The church supper recalls the joys of fellowship around a covered dish when time was not rushed and subsequent entertainment was wholesome and serene. It does not quite fit today's businessman who would rather watch tonight's TV episode of "The Man From U.N.C.L.E.," or the teen-ager who seeks a thrill at a frantic discotheque. The Quarterly Conference calls to mind a seasonal review of church affairs along the lines of a representative town meeting where duly elected officers have their full say. It does not quite fit today's rapid pace. The word "quarterly" is a misnomer since the conference may be held once or twice a year and is often attended only by the faithful whom the pastor is able to induce to come out of loyalty even though they think it may be dull!

Even Biblical imagery, as one would expect, is rural. Lambs and mustard seed, lilies of the field and vineyards, the blade and the full-grown ear call up to the imagination a rural setting that is not immediately familiar to urban man who deals in carburetors, stocks, mortgages, and advertising. At the very least the modern congregation has a prodigious task of reinterpreting the rural practices and imagery it has inherited if it is to make any relevant sense to the urban man of the twentieth century, no matter how far away from the inner city he may drive his car to the split-level house he calls home.

Fourth, the nature of rapid social change is attested by *the radically new expectations of mankind*. If we are witnessing speedy shifts in population growth, in communications, and in urbanization, we are witnessing no less significant shifts in the attitudes of men who out of seemingly phlegmatic and age-old passivity now burst into demands whose urgency is both strident and overpowering. Men expect as of right what their forefathers only a few years ago did not dream of.

The former great colonial powers have presided over the dissolution of their empires as former quiet subjects suddenly gained a vision of freedom and transformed the vision into reality. Young men in Asia today expect an education and bend efforts almost unknown in the West to fulfill their expectations. In Latin American countries poverty-stricken populations have accepted their lot for generations; but today they begin to move restlessly, sometimes violently, demanding that the privileges traditionally shared by the military, the large landowners, and the Roman Catholic hierarchy be spread out for the benefit of all. It is as though revolution is breathed in the air and must be actualized in concrete new expressions: a share in material prosperity, an opportunity to learn to read and write, a decent dwelling, and a measure of job security.

In our own country the Negro revolution is of the same stripe. After a century and more of second-class citizenship or worse, the

Negro today demands equality before the law, dignity of treatment, and economic opportunity equivalent to that of his white brother. Whether or not he should get these and other benefits is a totally irrelevant question: he expects them, he knows how to get them, and he will get them.

Characteristic of every such expectation is the search for a participation in authentic humanity. For whatever reasons, this is a day in which history witnesses a more massive and insistent expectation of the basic gifts and attributes of human selfhood than any other age. For twenty centuries the Christian church has spoken eloquently about the "abundant life" which should be open to every man. For most listeners during those centuries this could only mean some kind of spiritual abundance which would overflow the heart and make tolerable the sufferings of the age. Suddenly our age witnesses a solid expectation by great masses of men that the abundant life in its totality—material, mental, and spiritual—is conceivably within their grasp, and they eagerly rush into history to possess it.

Here the church may well find a genuine opportunity. May it not begin by interpreting this rising tide of expectations as intimately related to the activity of God in history? When masses of men seek out dignity and freedom, opportunities and knowledge, as never before, the very least the church in this day can do is to rejoice exceedingly and welcome the new world that has suddenly emerged.

A church that can join with Mary, the mother of Jesus, in repeating the Magnificat will rejoice at the new world before us:

> His name is Holy . . .
> the arrogant of heart and mind he has put to rout,
> he has torn imperial powers from their thrones,
>     but the humble have been lifted high.
> The hungry he has satisfied with good things,
>     the rich sent empty away. (Luke 1:49-53)

To share in this revolution of authentic humanity is to participate in the very prophecy our Lord used to characterize his whole ministry:

> The spirit of the Lord is upon me because he has anointed me;
> He has sent me to announce good news to the poor,
> To proclaim release for prisoners and recovery of sight for the blind;
> To let the broken victims go free,
> To proclaim the year of the Lord's favour. (Luke 4:18, 19)

## A Surging World

If rapid change is a fact of our world with which we have to deal, a closely allied second fact is the immense growth of power. Every society in every age has had to determine how power would be exercised, used, distributed, and controlled. The determination has been a political decision which has resulted in the greatest variety of political forms, from near-anarchy to empire, from city-states to totalitarian dictatorships, from socialist utopias to constitutional democracies. This has been essentially a quest of governmental forms that would serve to direct the use of power and control or mediate the conglomerate of varying lesser power centers within the governmental unit. The presence of power and the need for its orderly control is not new. What is new in the twentieth century is (1) the massive increase of power available to modern man, (2) the intensified search for new sources of power, and (3) the emergence of new centers of power.

Never before in mankind's history has so much power been so accessible to men and societies. As an individual I make daily use of all kinds of power my ancestors did not know existed. I awake in the morning and turn on a light which is made possible by controlled electric power. I drive to work in a car I cannot push more than a block but which, thanks to controlled mechanical power, takes me to my destination at whatever speed local laws deem appropriate. I eat pepped-up foods that promise to give me new energy and vitality. I use a telephone that makes use of electro-magnetic waves. I read a newspaper and submit, usually unknow-ingly, to the power of advertising. I deposit some money in a bank and thereby contribute to the flow of economic power in the com-munity. I pay taxes and thus help sustain the vast political power of my nation along with its military establishment, its adventures into space, and its experimentation with new laws that in turn are enforced upon my life. My world is surging with power.

The potential at man's command is greater than ever before. It opens up vistas of heart-warming hope. Illnesses that not long ago were a threat to my children and to me can be forgotten if we take the proper vaccinations. We no longer worry about typhoid fever, smallpox, polio, and diphtheria. Power over nature is gained increasingly to a point where man begins to think that any natural phenomenon may be subjected to his control and domination. The terrifying fact that accompanies this vast increase in power is that it carries with it the possibility of our total destruction. The atomic bombs dropped on Hiroshima and Nagasaki in 1945 were, by present-day standards, so weak and primitive that we can almost look back on them with nostalgia! The arsenal of thermonuclear weapons at man's disposal today is, we are told, perfectly capable of pulverizing the earth and terminating the human experiment on this planet.

Not satisfied with the sources of power already at our reach, man has embarked on the most intensive search for new sources of power. Whether it be in placid salt water, or in the sun's rays, or in protons, or in unknown elements, no effort is spared to wrest new knowledge out of nature which will result in new dimensions of power available to man and his society. This is not limited to the physical and material aspects of life, but to the mental and spiritual realms as well; so that power over behavior and child development, over social attitudes and political notions, over un-conscious wishes and subliminal desires, is sought unceasingly and found to an almost frightening degree. No less an authority than Dr. James B. Conant, former president of Harvard University, remarks that "the most dramatic, if not the most significant change in the scientific scene within the lifetime of many of us is the acceptance of the interconversion of matter and energy." [8] To my unscientific mind this idea suggests that there may be sources of power at the fingertips of humanity of which we do not even dream but which many of our fellowmen are bending every effort to uncover in our day.

With the growth of power and the search for new sources of power there comes a tremendous fluctuation in the centers of power. It is, for example, hard for us today to realize that the scientist's emergence into the center of power is extremely recent. Dr. Conant reminds us of this as he recalls two incidents of World War I. The first was the appointment of a Navy consultation board by President Wilson. Thomas Edison was the chairman. He was an inventor, not a scientist. A solitary physicist was added to the board because Edison had said to President Wilson, "We might have one mathematical fellow in case we have to calculate something out." [9] The second incident was the offer of the American Chemical Society to the Secretary of War, Newton Baker, of chemists who were ready to help as they could in the conflict. Secretary Baker was grateful for the gesture but explained that he had looked into the matter and had found that the War Department already had *a* chemist! Today a nation would not know how to wage war without physicists, chemists, and almost every variety of scientist as guides and full participants every step of the way.

On another level of power, the shift in its center is eloquently symbolized by the change in voting power within the United Nations General Assembly. On the eve of World War I there

---

[8] James B. Conant, *Modern Science and Modern Man*, Doubleday Anchor, 1952, pages 63, 64.
[9] *Ibid.*, pages 17-19.

were 63 independent states in the world, and at the beginning of World War II the number had grown a bit to 71. The United Nations was organized in 1945 with most of these nations as members. Then came the explosion of nation-states. From the end of World War II to 1964 over 50 new nations became politically independent. A recent report [10] (almost certainly inaccurate in late 1965 due to the emergence of new nations) indicates that towards the end of 1964 there were 120 independent nations. Fifty-five of these are in Europe and the Western Hemisphere, sixty-five in Asia, Africa, and Oceania. Translated into voting power in the U. N. General Assembly, where most of these nations are members, it is clear that the West is no longer in a dominant position. The balance of voting power has shifted radically. Only by virtue of the Security Council veto in the hands of the five "great powers" is the West able to conserve a shaky dominance, as three of those powers are the United States, Great Britain, and France, while the other two are Russia (in many ways a Western nation) and China (representative in fact, at this writing, of the relatively small island of Taiwan).

It is extremely difficult for the church to adjust to the world of power. What has a Christian congregation to do with growing power, new sources of power, and new centers of power? So much of the Christian mind-set shies away from a confrontation of the realities of power. We have heard that "in weakness there is strength," that "the meek shall inherit the earth," and that we must "love our enemies." To dirty our hands with involvement in power struggles, competitive power politics, thermonuclear power, or even nonviolent power appears to many as directly contrary both to the letter and the spirit of the gospel. The one power we would rely upon is the unmistakable power of the Holy Spirit. But if

---

[10] Bulletin of Office for Research, Commission on Ecumenical Mission and Relations of The United Presbyterian Church in the U.S.A., Vol. IV, No. 4, November 9, 1964.

there is any truth in the statement that God has thrown us into history and that the world in some way sets the agenda for the church, we are placed unavoidably in the midst of power realities which we cannot ignore. A town or city congregation that opens its eyes to the world immediately surrounding it is immediately conscious of all kinds of powers with which it will have to deal if it is to be anything other than an island to itself: the power of local business, the mayor and town governing bodies, the power of labor interests, and the power of community service organizations, to mention only a few related directly to the local scene. A rural congregation has comparable power entities with which to deal.

The involvement of the local congregations in power realities takes on its greatest implications when they consider their responsibility to the underprivileged of society. The church has never had any doubt, however it may have acted, that one of its major responsibilities was to the downtrodden and helpless. How it exercised such a responsibility may have varied considerably from time to time and place to place, but the responsibility never disappeared.

Increasingly Protestant Christians who have shied away from involvement in power struggles have come to agree with Dr. John C. Bennett, President of Union Theological Seminary in the City of New York, when he says that an important aspect of Christian social responsibility is the political organization of the victims of social injustice so that they can use their power to change conditions. The moment a congregation accepts this kind of responsibility, it is thrust potentially into the most agonizing decisions it can face, with all the ambiguities that any participant in power realities faces. But the only alternative is to eschew such participation, and to do so in this day is clearly a retreat from the implications of the gospel itself. Dr. Bennett elaborates on some of these implications:

The minister may play a provisional political role in these situations, since he is a visible spokesman for his own people who need his leadership. The ambiguities of this role are less than the ambiguities that surround the political silence of the minister in a homogeneous church that resists change, who allows the people to think that he agrees with them when he doesn't.

The church needs many ministers who identify themselves with the efforts of the poor to gain power to balance the thousands of ministers who, implicitly, give their blessing to the way the strong keep their power. There are no clear roles in this area.[11]

The point is that a congregation involved in mission, in the midst of a world saturated with power struggles and conflicts, many of them extremely creative in their end-results, must find the resources to deal both with the fact of power and with the ambiguities this dealing implies. In the search for meaningful involvement in power the congregation will find resources in the concept of Christian justice, and in the midst of ambiguities it will find strength and unity in Christian acceptance and forgiveness.

## A Secularized World

The world in which we believe God acts is a world which increasingly believes and acts as though God did not exist at all. To put it bluntly, for much of the world God is dead. We know that societies have existed in the past which centered their life around a particular religious concept. The Israel of the Old Testament was such a society. The medieval dominance of Roman Christianity in much of Europe provides another example. Our early American Puritan societies offer yet another. It is even possible to argue that in our very recent past our American society has been permeated

---

[11] John Bennett, "The Church and Power Conflicts," article published in *Christianity and Crisis*, March 22, 1965.

by a religious "establishment" of impressive proportions.[12] However, the shifting and surging world in which we live today is rapidly shedding any such ties to a religious base.

We hear more than one lamentation that we have moved into a "post-Christian world" or a "religiousless society" which is blamed, as often as not, on modern science or modern technology or both. Man has come into a new exhilarating sense of his own powers and potentialities and therefore feels no need of a supportive God to help him make his way in the world. If we wish, we can bemoan this fact or rail against it, but no one can seriously maintain that it is not a reality of our present world. The issue then becomes, "How do we deal with it?"

A first step is to try to understand secularization. Charles West reported on a consultation of university professors held at the Ecumenical Institute in Bossey, Switzerland, in 1959. The theme of the consultation was "The Meaning of the Secular." In this report secularization is defined as "the withdrawal of areas of thought and life from religious—and finally also from metaphysical—control, and the attempt to understand and live in these areas in the terms which they alone offer." This is a suggestive definition, for it does not specifically refer to Christianity (unless we take for granted that Christianity should control thought and life), nor does it rule out an understanding of the meaning of our history in terms which might well coincide with a Christian interpretation of that history. To Christians who are emotionally conditioned immediately to attack or disavow anything that can be termed "secular," almost as by a reflex action, it may come as a bit of a surprise that secularization might possibly be something that can be affirmed as good. We very easily contrast what is supposedly spiritual with what is supposedly secular. We are tempted to say the former is good and the latter is bad.

---

[12] See Peter Berger, *The Noise of Solemn Assemblies*, Doubleday & Company, Inc., 1961.

In the face of this it must come as a surprise to hear as eminent a Christian thinker of our day as Hans Hoekendijk say flatly that "we will not be able really to get alongside man in our modern world unless we begin to 'dereligionize' Christianity. Christianity is a secular movement, and this is basic for an understanding of it. . . . The coming of Jesus Christ in this modern world will be a secular event or it will not happen at all." [13] In what sense can this be true?

Merely as a matter of empirical observation, it can be recorded that most twentieth-century men do not resort to some hypothesis about the existence or power of God to explain either the nature of our world or the direction history is taking. There is a genuine sense that much of life as we know it has been liberated from a control that somehow comes from some outside God. Thus an article in *Time* magazine observes:

His lordship over the world has been threatened by every scientist who discovered a new natural law of organic growth, by every invention of man that safeguarded him against "act of God" disaster, by every new medicine that tamed a disease and solved another mystery of life. But it is the 20th century, the age of technological miracle, that has seen the triumph of the Enlightenment and the apparent banishment of God from the universe—even, thanks to Freud, from the human soul.[14]

Even non-Christian cultures which come under the impact of Western technological civilization, whatever their prior religious framework, witness the breakdown of transcendent explanations of the world, particularly among their youth, as man's science and power become evident. The result is a massive mental and spiritual revolution which is no less significant than any physical or technological change in our modern world. The props of explanation

---

[13] Quoted in an editorial in *Student World*, World Student Christian Federation, No. 1, 1963, Geneva.
[14] *Time* magazine, article entitled "The Servant Church," December 25, 1965, page 46.

and understanding have been knocked out from under many a civilization that depended on religious faith for ultimate meaning; and whatever may have replaced them, if anything has, we are confronted with an entirely new world we have not been adequately prepared to meet.

On the other hand, one can be grateful that much which previously passed as an explanation of the universe based on faith is now seen to be a rather false religiosity. At its worst, the supposedly religious nature of a culture has been little more than a veneer which has maintained the illusion that we are religious, no matter what our real motivations and ethical decisions. We can pretend we are religious by repeating every hour on the hour that we are "One Nation Under God" or by insisting that every meeting, whether a Rotary luncheon or the inauguration of our President, begin with a prayer. However valid these acts may be in themselves, too easily they deceive us into a more infatuated concept of ourselves and of our religious nature than can be defended on any objective examination of our real motivations, actions, and decisions.

To the extent that the overlay of religiosity is torn away from us by the secular revolution of our times so that the truth about ourselves and our culture can be seen, we have been beneficiaries of a great service. Secularization has helped Christianity see itself for what it is and for what it is not. It imposes on Christianity a measure of honesty that too often we have not accepted. Thus one question can readily be asked: is not secularization the work of God himself? To what extent is the very secular revolution of our time, so criticized by many who defend things spiritual, part of God's action in history which the Christian church should acknowledge and welcome?

Add to this the fact that secularization points up the tangential and marginal nature of much of our Christian practice. The moment Christianity becomes one religion alongside another religion, as so easily modern man conceives it, the central nerve of Christian faith is cut off from the life man must lead in this world. If Christianity is admittedly one religion, among many, which is competitively trying to gain converts at a faster rate than any other religion, it is admitting from the outset that the Christian understanding of God, man, and history is somehow applicable to those who call themselves Christians but not to others who reject Christianity or who choose some other creed. It is against this kind of compartmentalization that we can understand Dr. Hoekendijk's call to "de-religionize" Christianity.

The issue we raise here, without attempting to explore the inner dynamics of today's secular revolution, is whether our world's secularization can be seen as in some way God's action in history, which means the Christian congregation should seek to participate in it. Some Christians today believe this is precisely the case. For example, one writes:

Wherein lies the true secularity of the church? It is in believing and acting out realistically the message that Jesus Christ is not only the Lord of the church but is also the Lord of General Motors and the Democratic Party and is working quite outside the church as such, to fulfill the reconciliation of the world.[15]

An even more striking argument is that propounded by Arend Th. van Leeuwen, a European theologian, who argues in a recent book [16] that the process of secularization has its roots in Judaeo-Christian history. Western technological civilization, he maintains, is a direct and logical outgrowth of Biblical history and faith. This Western technology has moved irresistibly across the world, pene-

---

[15] Gayraud S. Wilmore, *The Secular Relevance of the Church,* The Westminster Press, Philadelphia, 1962, page 21.
[16] Arend Th. van Leeuwen, *Christianity in World History,* Edinburgh House Press, 1964.

trating every culture, in a process that cannot be reversed or halted. The net result is a worldwide secularization the roots of which are in Biblical faith. True Christianity is thereby present incognito in all world cultures touched by this irresistible process, and we who claim to be part of the Christian church must reorient our enitre mind-set to see how we might participate in God's work in the secularization process, if in fact is it God's work. Van Leeuwen adds:

It is helpful to make a clear distinction between secularization and secularism. The first is a continuing historical process, the second a fixed and absolutized ideology with a tendency towards pagan or nihilistic totalitarianism. The relation of the Christian church to the advancing history of secularization is in any event a positive one; it carries responsibility for it and is intimately concerned and involved with what that process brings in its train, with all that it so richly promises and with its appalling threats and dangers.[17]

This raises immense questions for the Christian congregation. We may find that this line of argument is not altogether satisfying to us. To deal with a "Christianity incognito" may be to chase a will-o'-the-wisp. It may provide little or no basis for a self-understanding of the church and its mission. It may dissolve the distinctiveness Christian faith presumably has, and it even may raise a serious question as to the finality of Christ. Nevertheless, if there is some truth in this, what does a local congregation do with it?

At a minimum it must mean that the local congregation can look out upon its world, whether it be near or far away, with the knowledge that it does not have to assault the world in the name of God as though God were not already in that world. Structures of secularity may provide an honesty for the life of man which presumed religious structures of the past did not. The congrega-

[17] *Ibid.*, page 334.

tion may well see its major call as a call to work within the very secular structures God has raised up around it, attempting to help modern men within these structures to acknowledge the Lord who, unknowingly to us all, brought us face to face with secularization. The radical reorientation this may mean for many a Christian congregation is scarcely imaginable.

How far we may be from this change of mind can be judged as we compare an average American congregation's life against the words of one of our modern prophets. Dietrich Bonhoeffer has articulated as well as any the importance of an affirmation of the secularization process as the realm within which Christians are to act without apology and without resort to a deceptively "religious" faith. Writing to a child, Bonhoeffer says:

Our Christianity today will be confined to praying for and doing right by our fellow men. Christian thinking, speaking, and organization must be reborn out of this praying and this action. By the time you are grown up, the form of the church will have changed beyond recognition. . . . The day will come when men will be called again to utter the word of God with such power as will change and renew the world. It will be a new language, which will horrify men, and yet overwhelm them by its power. . . . Until then the Christian cause will be a silent and hidden affair, but there will be those who pray and do right and wait for God's own time.[18]

Perhaps there is no more perplexing question for a Christian congregation than to ask how it may relate, in a "silent and hidden" way to the secularized world in which, we suspect, God is himself at work in a "silent and hidden" way. Perplexing as it may be, there is probably no search in which a congregation may engage which might be potentially more productive of fidelity to the innermost meaning of the Christian faith.

---

[18] Dietrich Bonhoeffer, *Letters and Papers from Prison*, SCM Press, 1954, pages 140-141.

## A SUFFERING WORLD

The reality of widespread physical human suffering is vitrually incomprehensive to most American congregations. Our own comforts close off our understanding. Yet it remains one of the predominant facts of our time. If God works in human history in today's world, he is surely present in the midst of this most acute and painful suffering. In the United States we are engaged in a War on Poverty designed to reduce some of the physical suffering of our own nation. We define poverty as the economic state of a family that has an income of less than $3000 per year. Appalachia is a symbol of this poverty for us. We seek out ways of raising our minimum standards of living. We are concerned with human suffering, but the magnitude of our world's suffering is brought home to us with a force we can scarcely understand when we hear, for example, that half the world goes to bed hungry every night, or that 56 percent of the population of Peru earns less than $54.00 per year, or that thousands of families in Calcutta have absolutely no covered dwelling of any kind and must spend a lifetime existing, sleeping, living, and starving on a staked-out piece of uncovered sidewalk or sheer dirt. Anyone who travels with eyes open to see the misery of today's world is likely to come to a point where the immensity of it all simply becomes overwhelming and hence incomprehensible and uncommunicable.

As I recall only the bits of it that I have seen—the refugee lepers' community living in squalor in a destroyed building in Pusan, Korea; the infamous slums of Lima, Peru; the "rat-towns" of Uruguay; the "misery villages" of Argentina; the *favellas* of Rio de Janeiro stacked up on steep mountain slopes overlooking plush Copacabana—and know that millions live in worse conditions than any I have witnessed, the enormity of it defies description.

There comes a point when nothing is gained by piling grim statistic upon grim statistic to augment the picture of horror. The mind recoils and shuts out what imagination cannot envision. We are apt to respond emotionally to the nature of this suffering if we see it personalized in a symbolic individual who we know is as real as ourselves: the new mother in Northeast Brazil who knows her chances of keeping her baby are very slim, since every twenty seconds a child dies in that area due to lack of elemental medical care; the grimy child in India with an overextended belly who reaches out a skinny hand to beg for any crust at all; the Congolese youth who fingers a revolver for the first time and wonders whether it might not get him his first taste of affluence, since every other means has been barred to him. Even to skirt the edges of this vast sea of human suffering is to court insensitivity and escape.

Alongside and intertwined with the physical suffering is the less visible but often more excruciating mental and spiritual suffering from which no group is immune. We read that divorce rates in our own nation went up in 1964 from 5 percent to 8 percent, probably due to early marriages.[19] We hear that thirty thousand Negro elevator operators in New York City alone have been thrown into unemployment as automated elevators have rendered their services unnecessary.[20] We are reminded repeatedly of the many ways in which our fellow citizens try to escape from boredom or worse by countless varieties of narcotics, tranquilizers, and pep pills, often marketed at a hundred times their value. The assaults that minority groups endure every day upon their basic human dignity, as silently they are turned away from full participation in the life enjoyed by the majority, contribute to the deep inner hurt which lacerates the soul and for which no healing salve is adequate. Millions bear in silence the burden of meaninglessness which turns sour or tasteless almost any human endeavor and leads to the passivity or sullen rebellion that distorts all values. So on and on.

---

[19] *Changing Times,* The Kiplinger Magazine, February 1965, page 5.
[20] See article, "A Cry from the Dispossessed," by Whitney M. Young, Jr., *The Christian Century,* December 9, 1964, pages 1524-1527.

Is this part of God's work in history? Is this world, infused as it is with suffering of incalculable dimensions, the outcome of God's purposes? We can more easily believe that rapid social change, surging new power, and a secular revolution are related to God's doing than we can accept the idea that God is responsible for all this misery. And, of course, we do not have to believe that God is responsible for suffering, even when much of it remains unexplainable to us. What we must affirm as Christians is that the God who revealed himself in Jesus Christ has shown himself to be a God who identifies himself intimately with the world's suffering. He is present and very much at work in what we might call the "structures of suffering."

Theologically the doctrine of Christ's incarnation bespeaks an identification of God with our human condition, which is meaningless if it does not include the realm of suffering. Practically, as a matter of experience, Christians testify that in the moments of worst suffering, physical or otherwise, the one greatest factor that made the difference between meaningful and meaningless suffering was the realization of the presence of the Holy Spirit, which at least by their experience was something more than a psychological trick to help them endure the unendurable.

If God is thus identified in some way with the structures of suffering, and if the world sets the agenda for the congregation, a major concern of any local congregation that takes seriously the needs around it will be its participation with God in his mission in the midst of suffering. The church is called to relieve and prevent unnecessary suffering and to identify with those who suffer insofar as such identification is humanly possible.

A first problem is simply the awareness the congregation must have of the suffering that surrounds it. This could seem to be relatively easy, given the ample information that even our daily newspapers carry about the world's suffering. But the very magnitude of this suffering calls for some kind of focusing. At the least a congregation will want to keep closely and clearly before it the nature of a particular suffering which it can help in some measure to relieve. Whether this focus will be a nearby slum, a mental hospital, a prison, a marriage counseling center, a migrant labor camp, or some other point where men and women appear to carry a heavy burden of suffering, only each congregation can determine for itself.

In recent years many congregations have come to a new awareness of human suffering as they have taken seriously the injustices that racial minorities endure in our country. Genuine concern for human need at one point tends to widen our concern for those who suffer in other areas beyond those most familiar to us. To become aware in depth of some point of human suffering and to try to feel the import of this suffering as one's own is a long step in the direction of both compassion and service.

Beyond this there is the nature of the congregation's response to the need encountered. Specific, individual acts of human kindness and mercy never go out of date and always have their own validity. Christian concern for suffering humanity seeks, however, not only to be palliative to relieve suffering that has already come about, but it seeks as well to prevent unnecessary suffering before it occurs. This is one point at which the Christian congregation comes hard up against its understanding of justice as the concrete expression in human relationships of Christian love.

It is very clear in the Gospels that Jesus identified himself with the victims of injustice. It is therefore appropriate for a Christian congregation to do the same, unpopular as this may sometimes be. This identification takes on large measures of ambiguity when it means identification with the underprivileged by participation in movements of a political nature to obtain the recognition of rights and the improvement of unjust situations.

Protestant Christians are not noted, as a group, for participation in nonviolent demonstrations, labor picket lines, protest meetings against gambling interests, or for community pressures upon a negligent school board. Many honorable exceptions come to mind, but too often it has been our stance to relieve suffering which has occurred rather than to seek to prevent by organized pressure the injustice which eventuates in suffering.

A Protestant bishop, struck by the appalling conditions of injustice in one Latin American country, raised the very relevant question as to whether the Methodist church in that nation was identified in the minds of the populace with the victims of injustice. The answer came back that although some Methodists were active in movements to eradicate the causes of injustice as these were understood, nevertheless the church as a whole rather represented a bourgeois middle-class mentality that was not really identified with the underprivileged. It sought instead to rise out and away from the suffering of the lower economic classes. The bishop reminded his listeners in that country of a phrase attributed to President Woodrow Wilson to the effect that "society disintegrates from the top down." He suggested that if the church sought to identify its future with the upper middle class and higher economic groups the day might well come when Latin American revolutionary social forces would sweep through that nation, as in fact they are already doing, wiping out those at the top. The growing political power of the underprivileged would simply bypass the church and render it totally irrelevant.

One final comment about the identification of the congregation with suffering is in order. There is a real sense in which a single congregation is powerless to deal with massive misery save as it participates in organized response to suffering in league with many other similar congregations.

What can a church of five hundred members in Kansas do when suddenly it senses an urge to help relieve suffering caused by an earthquake in Chile or in Alaska? In and of itself there is little it can do except as it combines with many other congregations with similar concerns. Here one becomes aware of the immense validity of organized Christian agencies which provide the channels for meeting the massive kind of need here suggested. The tremendous contribution of Church World Service and of the Methodist Committe for Overseas Relief, to mention but two of them, is incalculable. One is tempted into impatience with any who would throw overboard all church structures as we now know them and include in the overthrow such agencies which meet a magnitude of need that no new congregational grouping exclusively concerned with the tangible mission at its doorstep can begin to meet. A measure of Christian comprehensiveness in response to human suffering is the willingness of a congregation to respond with empathy and generosity to the wide world of need it cannot see with its eyes but which it can serve with its open hand and heart as it joins with many others eager to do the same.

## A Searching World

Finally, our twentieth-century world is very much a searching world. What it is searching for is not easy to define. It is a bit presumptuous for Christians to assume, as so frequently happens, that the whole world is searching for precisely the answers Christians are ready to give. Even if there is truth, as I believe there is, in the affirmation that the resources of the gospel are sufficient to meet man's deepest need, it does not of necessity follow that mankind is embarked upon a process of discovery that inevitably issues in satisfaction by the Christian faith. On the contrary, we see any number of thoughtful men who today seriously study the Christian faith and find it wanting. We may not agree with their reasons or their methods of study, but we cannot dismiss their sincerity or their honesty. A man like the late Albert Camus delves deeply into the nature of the universe and of man's being and comes up with the conclusion that the whole thing is "absurd." He speaks not for himself alone, but for a whole generation of our time

107

that wants to know some measure of truth but in all honesty finds that truth exceedingly difficult to ferret out.

Our purpose here is not to analyze all the various types of searches in which our world engages. We have already mentioned the search for new sources of power. There is the formidable scientific research of our time which wrests from matter and energy secrets hitherto undreamed. There is the quest of human dignity, founded on expectations that our technological civilization makes plausible. There is the urgent search for national and international peace. There is the silent but persistent search for meaning which does not content itself with the "absurd" but believes some kind of significance can be extricated from the life we know and experience. Whether the search is deliberate investigation of the scholar or the half-conscious yearning in the depths of a human soul, no one doubts that twentieth-century man is thrown into this search with a great new urgency.

On the front page of *The New York Times* on almost any day the search is compellingly evident. At random I take the front page of the *Times* on Sunday, May 2, 1965 and find that the United Nations Security Council is about to meet to search for a solution for an international incident heightened in its delicacy by the landing of U.S. Marines in the Dominican Republic; that a victory has been obtained in the search for new speed as the YF-12A experimental plane set a new world speed record of over 2,000 miles per hour; that while every two minutes someone in the United States dies of cancer, in that same two-minute period others spend more than $700 to try to understand cancer and search for its cure; that a search for new means of crime prevention is on as closed circuit television units are used on New York's subways to locate criminals; and, less important, that the owners of a horse named Lucky Debonair were successful in their search for the Kentucky Derby crown, the New York Yankees won, and, as expected, the New York Mets failed again in their search for an occasional victory!

108

The point of this recital simply is that man's mental stance today is one of continual and undeterred searching. The very process of investigation, analysis, expectation of new understanding, and quest for improved relationships with nature and among men seems to be in the very air we breathe. So present is it that we take it for granted as the natural state of man and find it just a bit trite to have it lifted up for special attention. But when we think of the congregations which seek new forms of responding to the world around them, this fact is of crucial significance. It means at a minimum that the church should recognize, as it deals with twentieth-century men, that it is dealing with a mind-set that is not conditioned to accept pat answers. It means that the congregation deals with men as searching men or runs the risk of losing them altogether by minimizing or overlooking the quest in which they are engaged.

The question the congregation will want to ask is whether the searching world is expressive of God's activity in history. Is God active in today's world in that he moves men to seek for new discoveries in science and human relations, new understanding of truths as yet but dimly seen or not even imagined? Were the church to conclude that this is simply man's curiosity, unaffected by God's design, it might well draw the conclusion that the congregation's life can be lived on the margins of the human quest. But this is pretty hard to accept. If God is at all related to contemporary history, he must surely be related to the thousand and one ways in which men seek out new truth or new understanding of the truth. God who, we believe, reveals truth also moves men to seek the truth he has for them. The energy and drive behind the search for new truths in our day, seen in this light, may well be a most heartening sign of the very near presence of the God who in our day is stimulating us all to seek truth in history more fervently than ever before.

If a congregation can believe this, every legitimate search for truth is its ally, and every illegitimate twisting of man's search is its concern. How to participate with God in his activity in a searching world will be a major question. On the one hand the congregation will doubtless want to delve into the meaning of listening, in order to know what the primary searches of modern man are. Here we may be helped by the way in which Christian university students conceive their role in the university community, a world in which the search for truth and new knowledge is fundamental. In 1964 a group of students of the World Student Christian Federation, in attempting to state the meaning of Christian presence, wrote the following:

When we say "presence," we say that we have to get into the midst of things even when they frighten us. Once we are there, we may witness fearlessly to Christ if the occasion is given: we may also have to be silent . . . we trust that while present we will be given new words or an authentic silence.

On the other hand, the congregation will increasingly sense that the way to identification with the search for truth is in dialogue with those who search rather than in a one-sided statement of what appear to be Christian answers that never really engage the questions being asked. You and I may agree with a Sunday-morning preacher who states outright that "Christ is the answer to every problem," but the twentieth-century non-Christian who is involved in a search for truth in complex areas of human endeavor will not be so sure. He will be particularly doubtful if the same preacher cannot speak with him, instead of to him, about the ambiguities, the half-truths, the veiled assumptions, and the questions that are present as much in the world of the searcher as in the world of the preacher. In a word, to participate with God in the history of a searching world entails a humility for everyone concerned, particularly for the congregation that covets a measure of relevance to its surrounding environment.

110

The world in which we are claimed by God to live is shifting, surging, secularized, suffering, and searching. It is that and much more, but for the Christian it is supremely a world in which God is active, even though we cannot discern much of the mystery of that activity. As such, then, it is a world we welcome, even with all its uncertainties, threats, and confusions.

An anecdote is told about a man who decided to sell his farmhouse. He put the sale in the hands of a real estate agent, who prepared a glowing description of the property designed to appeal to any buyer. The man selling the house read the description and was so impressed that he commented, "That is the house I always dreamed of buying!" He cancelled the sale and stayed where he was. We may be tempted more than once to check out of this frustrating world; but if we begin to see it as the arena of God's activity in history, exciting and demanding, we relish the opportunity to be a part of it and share in God's mission.

We sing, "This is my Father's world." A congregation seeking new life seeks forms of witnessing service that respond readily to what our Father appears to be doing in his world, a world we receive with profound joy because we know to whom it belongs.

\* \* \*

## Questions for Discussion

1. What does it mean to you that "the world sets the agenda for the church"?
2. What major changes in our twentieth-century world are so important for your congregation that you must give serious thought and time to a consideration of your response to them?
3. It is often said that today every man is an urban man, no matter where he lives. In what sense is this true?
4. How does your congregation deal with the development of new centers of power in your community?

5. If we live in a secularized world, in what sense does God call us to be secular men and women? Are there "Christian secular structures" in our society which we may welcome as indicative of God's activity in our modern world?

6. As you think of your local community, what are the major searches upon which your congregation should embark?

## chapter V

## CLAIMED BY THE WORD

*Renewed structures must be responsive to God's Word as revealed in Scripture. This Word portrays a variety of congregational forms in constant change, oriented to the outsider. They are to be orderly and infused with genuine hope.*

We have considered some of the implications of the statement that "the world sets the agenda for the church." This is a helpful and stimulating concept, but by itself it is incomplete. An equally fruitful, and I believe correct, statement is that "the Word sets the agenda for the church." To this we turn now.

In no sense need we counterpose one idea to the other. Both are meaningful, and they readily complement each other. God's Word, revealed to man, comes to us in the midst of the world. God's world is the arena for the incarnation of God's Word.

As we consider the nature of the Christian church, its mission and task, as well as its structure, we are driven directly to the Word of God, which determines from the first the basic realities with which we deal and sets the framework and meaning of our response. This Word of God is God's act in history, his revelation by whatever means he chooses, his incarnation in Jesus Christ, and his participation in man's history, to which in a very special way the Scriptures testify. John begins: "When all things began, the Word already was. The Word dwelt with God, and what God was, the Word was" (John 1:1). This Word "became flesh" in Jesus

Christ, in whom we see "His glory, such glory as befits the Father's only Son, full of grace and truth" (John 1:14).

We often speak of the Bible as the "Word of God." This is an understandable and justifiable statement, provided we do not limit our concept of God's Word to a written or printed word, or to some phraseology presumably divinely inspired. Scriptures are the Word of God in that they record, and witness to, the eternal Word—God's act—which in a decisive and determinative way has broken upon man and his world. Because of what God has done in Christ and in history, a record of which is preserved for us in the writings of Scripture, we turn to the Bible for a renewed understanding of God himself and also of ourselves in the world.

## FOCUS ON THE CONGREGATION

The particular focus of our inquiry here is what we may learn from the Scriptures concerning the congregation. This opens up for us the much discussed question of the exact nature of the church, which has been analyzed and researched in great detail by competent scholarship. Our purpose here cannot be to review this mass of scholarly study, but rather to point up some of the insights that the Scriptures provide for us with particular reference to the missionary nature of the congregation and the forms that the congregation adopts as it carries on its mission.

The Greek word *ecclesia,* which we usually translate as "church" or as "congregation," is a much used word in the New Testament, and it also appears in the Greek translations of the Hebrew Old Testament word *quahal,* used to describe the assembly of the people of Israel. Paul uses the word some sixty times in his letters alone. Without attempting a detailed philological study, as persons seeking out the "missionary structure of the congregation" we can find some fascinating and thought provoking usages of the word *ecclesia* which may help to enlarge our idea of what God claims us to be in the congregation.

For example, has it ever occurred to you that the word *ecclesia,* for which you and I use "congregation" or "church," is equally applicable to a mob? It is not likely that in our common parlance we will picture a student mob scene in Korea or an out-of-control political rally in Argentina as an *ecclesia.* In our modern terms there seems to be nothing "ecclesiastical" about them! Yet something akin to this is described by the word in Acts 19:29-41. The town clerk on that occasion was overwhelmed by the disturbance of the *ecclesia* to a point where he remonstrated, "We certainly run the risk of being charged with riot for this day's work" (Acts 19:40). The point is that an *ecclesia* is first of all an assembly of people.

The purpose for which men, women, and children join together is highly important, but we dare not make too much of the fact that the church is "ecclesiastical," for at least in early New Testament times the word was a bit ambiguous, to say the least! We shall see that the Christian community took over this word and reshaped it, giving it new meaning; but it is well to remember at the outset the humility of origin of our term for the church. In the Greek world the word had a strong political connotation. It was the convened assembly of the citizens of a city-state's democratic way of life. Nothing was more thoroughly secular and political than an Athenian *ecclesia.*

## CALLED BY GOD FOR A PURPOSE

The Christian community moved on from this general meaning to a more specific concept tied to the kind of assembly in which they saw themselves participating. The crucial new element in the transformation of the meaning of the *ecclesia* was the introduction of the idea, held to strongly and most significant for us today, that a Christian assembly, a church or congregation, is summoned together by God himself. A Christian *ecclesia* is therefore not something that just happens because two or three or ten thousand of us decide to come together of our own wills to form a new fellowship or a more successful organization. The distinctive feature of any Christian church or congregation of which we are a part is that God brought us together. God claims us as a group. There is a wealth of New Testament evidence to this effect. As William Barclay has put it:

In essence, therefore, the Church, the *ekklēsia,* is a body of people, not so much assembling because they have chosen to come together, but assembling because God has called them to himself; not so much assembling to share their own thoughts and opinions, but assembling to listen to the voice of God.[1]

Closely allied to this is the accompanying idea that when God calls an assembly together, he does not do so without a clear purpose. That is to say, God's call to us to join in an assembly is part of his major purpose in history, part of the mission in which he is involved. We are brought together by him solely for mission, a mission which takes place in the world, a mission in which God is the chief Missioner. A careful study along this line is Johannes Blauw's, *The Missionary Nature of the Church.*[2] After a detailed analysis he concludes:

The Church which has been chosen out of the world is chosen for this end—that she performs for the world the service of giving witness to the Kingdom of God which has come and is coming in Jesus Christ. . . .

There is no other Church than the Church *sent* into the world, and there is no other mission than that of the Church of Christ. . . missionary work is not just one of its activities, but the *criterion for all its activities.*[3]

---

[1] William Barclay, *A New Testament Wordbook,* SCM Book Club, Chicago, 1955, page 35.
[2] Johannes Blauw, *The Missionary Nature of the Church,* McGraw-Hill Book Company, Inc., New York, 1962.
[3] *Ibid.,* pages 120-122.

Thus we see the church or congregation as an assembly, called together by God, for a missionary purpose.

It is well to note in passing that the word *ecclesia* never in the New Testament refers to a building! Our modern quick equation of a church with a particular edifice has no New Testament basis whatever. Special buildings for congregational groups probably did not appear until sometime in the third century. One need not jump from this New Testament fact to the conclusion that buildings are useless or contrary to the purposes of a church, but it is worth noting that vigorous churches existed and grew with immense vitality without a single building which was thought of as, or called, a church. The variety of places in which congregational groups met was great, but mainly these gatherings took place in homes, with the extensive development of "house-churches," such as the congregation in the house of Aquila and Prisca (1 Cor. 16:19), or Nymphas (Col. 4:15), and of Philemon (Philem. 2).

What guidance does the New Testament provide for a determination of the kind of congregational forms we may use today? If the New Testament is to be of substantial help to us in our search for renewed and renewing congregational structures for our day, this is a highly important question. It would appear that the answer, or answers, to that question may be quite disappointing to the man who would like a distinct blueprint to follow, but at the same time they may be quite relevant and suggestive for the person who is wrestling with the forms of the church's witness in our time. The contemporary nature of the New Testament, written in a time so dissimilar from our twentieth century, is notable.

## The Variety of New Testament Forms

First, the New Testament confronts us with *a great variety of congregational forms*. The diversity is striking. Is there such a thing as a New Testament structure of the congregation? Almost certainly not.

*The Jewish Christian Form.* In Jerusalem, the people of the congregation were closely tied to the Jewish temple (Acts 3:1). Here they brought their gifts (Matthew 5:23). Here they took vows related to Jewish practices (Acts 21:23, 24). The Mosaic law was observed (Galatians 2:12). The Sabbath was kept (Matthew 24:20). Circumcision was accepted as necessary for Jewish Christians (Acts 21:21). There were clear rules tied in with Jewish disciplinary practice (Matthew 18:15-18). There were elders with special responsibilities (Acts 21:18). The structures grew out of familiar practices, and the strictures of Jewish congregational life were quite severe. It can be argued that the proximity of these earliest Christian congregations to the heart of Jewish life and faith, a proximity both in time and space, made it only natural for them to carry over Jewish practices and structures into the newly emerging Christian congregational groups. Surely this was the case.

The only point to be made here is that this was one distinctive form of Christian congregational life, in which such men as Peter and James took full part. It was one kind of congregational response in early Christianity.

*The Pauline Type.* Quite a different type of congregational response appears in the churches that developed out of the ministry of the Apostle Paul. Here the emphasis was on the indwelling of the Spirit of Christ. Members of the congregation were characterized by possessing this Spirit (Romans 8:9). Whereas in Jerusalem there were elders, one does not find in Paul's early churches a difference between elders and laity. Particularly able or devoted leaders deserve recognition, but there is no indication of a special ordination for them (I Cor. 16:15-18, I Thess. 5:12, 13). The Corinthian congregations, which gave Paul such headaches, were congregations made up of "saints" (some of whom well qualify as disorderly sinners) and whose ebullience made for the most fluid kinds of structures. Central to any form was God's love (I

118

Cor. 13). Prophecy, sacrifice, and erudition meant nothing in God's congregation unless motivated, leavened, and expressed in God's love.

Here is a form of congregational life that lays much stress on the freedom of man and the church before God, a freedom in Christ for a congregation led by the Spirit.

*The Johannine Form.* Another picture emergies in the Johannine literature. Here an emphasis is placed on knowledge, albeit a knowledge of God (I John 2:13 ff.). The congregation proceeds on its understanding of what God has done in Christ, revealing himself and opening up eternal life (I John 5:20, 21). Not just any spirit may intrude upon the congregation; they are to "test the spirits" and discern whether they are from God or not (I John 4:1-6).

The congregation is that group in which the Spirit dwells (I John 3:24), and in this there is close similarity to Paul. Knowledge of the truth yields initiation into the life of the congregation by which the member dwells in the truth (I John 2:20, 27).

These are but three different forms of congregational life, not wholly distinct one from the other, for through each of them runs the central thread of response to God's action in Christ and the profound desire to be faithful to God. A central unity is present which ultimately led them all to take the path of martyrdom as a consequence of their witness to Jesus Christ, but clearly there was no one congregational form which could be labeled Christian. Even in what might be called the more conservative group, the Jerusalem Christians, there was a vast amount of freedom. Members of the community could baptize (Acts 8:38, 9:18). There was not great emphasis on officialdom (Matthew 23: 8-12), but importance is placed on humility (Matthew 18:4), service (Matthew 20:26), and lowliness (Matthew 23:12).[4]

---

[4] An illuminating article on these contrasts is Ed. Schweizer, "The Local Church and the Universal Church," *The Ecumenical Review*, Vol. VIII, No. 3, April 1956, pages 254 ff.

## CAPACITY FOR CHANGE

Secondly, the church forms we see in the New Testament are *in constant change*. No form is sacred and impervious to development. This is what one might expect in the early stages of any movement. It is also to be expected as Christian groups with varying modes of life come into touch with one another. Paul goes to Jerusalem to settle some differences that have arisen between Christian groups (Acts 15) and obtains a conciliatory statement from the Jerusalem leaders that indicates a readiness for change on their part. The joy with which Paul's churches receive the news implies a willingness to conform to the instructions given, which would mean adaptations of life and custom for them as well.

The flexibility of congregational structures is evident in much of the New Testament. From the less defined, almost amorphous church life of the early years following the ministry of Jesus, to the well organized church structures that developed by the time the epistles to Timothy and Titus were written, there was considerable change. The church was open to change and remarkably unhampered by any conviction that change should be avoided.

We may look back nostalgically and imagine that the lack of a developed Christian tradition allowed the kind of experimentation and pioneering our present structures so easily inhibit, but it is well to recall that many early Christians came out of the tradition-laden history of Judaism. They found in the gospel a new freedom which carried over not only to personal life and decision but also to the realm of corporate community life. In the deepest sense the freedom with which Christ makes us free allows a congregation, aware of this freedom and its corresponding responsibility, to respond to God's action with changes of great import in its corporate life and thus to meet developing new situations while maintaining a deep faithfulness to the gospel.

## Forms Oriented to the Outsider

Third, much of what we see in New Testament church forms indicates that these *forms are oriented to what might be called the "outsider."* [5] Jesus kept the Samaritan outsider and the publican constantly in mind. In the Pauline churches the whole thrust was towards the gentiles who were outside the church. Paul is very blunt about this when he discusses the practice of speaking in tongues, a practice which may have been meaningful to an "in-group" of Christians but which was gibberish and incomprehensible to the outsider. His words are worth quoting: "So if the whole congregation is assembled and all are using the 'strange tongues' of ecstasy, and some uninstructed persons or unbelievers should enter, will they not think you are mad?" (I Cor. 14:23). Or again, in the same connection: "Suppose you are praising God in the language of inspiration: how will the plain man who is present be able to say 'Amen' to your thanksgiving, when he does not know what you are saying? Your prayer of thanksgiving may be all that could be desired, but it is no help to the other man" (I Cor. 14: 16, 17).

This doctrine leads Eduard Schweizer to say, "The man from outside, the fringe member or gentile, is for Paul the proper yardstick by which the whole proclamation must be measured." [6]

The implications of this concern for the church today are most suggestive. The modern congregation should determine its life in terms of its mission to the outsider. The outsider will be the yardstick by which the validity of congregational structures is judged. Here the Word is telling us that "the world does set the agenda for the church." Some examples of what this may mean may be helpful.

---

[5] John Fleming and Ken Wright, *op. cit.,* refer to this theme briefly, pages 41-43.
[6] Eduard Schweizer, *Church Order in the New Testament,* SCM Press, London, 1961, page 28.

Some time ago a young woman was invited to attend a meeting of the local Woman's Society of Christian Service. The society in question is active and carries on an acceptable program. It raises a good deal of money and counts among its membership many able and educated women. The woman was invited to attend her first society meeting. Already she had been attending church services regularly. After sitting through an hour-long business session which dealt with seemingly interminable reports of attendance figures of the various circles and a hassle over the forthcoming bazaar, she was ill-prepared to listen very attentively to the main speaker of the evening, who by then had little chance to make a significant impact on anyone. The visitor came away from the meeting commenting that this was not for her. She felt her time could be more profitably used elsewhere. Whatever defense one may think of for the conduct of that meeting, and there could be many, the fact remained that it had not been geared to the needs and interests of a curious outsider who that day might have been won in the best sense, but instead was lost to that society and the genuine contribution it might make to her life.

Henry Lacy, area executive secretary for India and Nepal in the World Division of the Board of Missions of The Methodist Church, traveled recently in India and had, as a plane travel companion, a distinguished Sikh gentleman with high responsibility in the Planning Commission of the Indian Government. Mr. Lacy inquired, upon being told that this man wanted to employ Christians in his work, whether or not this was not a bit hazardous in that the Christians might try to propagate their faith. The unexpected answer was, "No, this is no problem, we cannot understand their preaching anyway!" The language of the Christians, meaningful in their own "in-group," apparently was not communicating anything to persons like this Sikh gentleman, and, to that degree, was not reaching the "outsider."

Lest these examples point too easily to the failures of others, I recall a rather recent speech I gave to a Methodist Aldersgate Service in Buenos Aires, Argentina. I chose to recount something of the history and meaning of John Wesley's ministry, relating it (I thought) to the witness of our church today. The next day a friendly but forthright missionary told me that he had brought a communist friend to that service, hopeful that something would be said that might speak to the communist mind. The missionary's remark about my speech was: "It was a wonderful speech, but totally irrelevant! We cannot give ourselves the luxury these days of merely talking to ourselves." The communist had been unimpressed. The outsider had apparently not been the yardstick by which that speech was conceived.

## Who Is the Outsider?

One further dimension of this idea is raised by the question, "Who is the outsider?" The foregoing discussion implicitly presumes that we who call ourselves Christian belong to an "in-group" from within which we can talk to the outside world. This image fits very well with our picture, alluded to earlier, of God working through the church in the world. But if God is seen working in the world and calling the church to participate in that work, then there is a real sense in which we are all outsiders. It is healthy corrective to some of our presumptions as Christians to remember that the dividing line between those who participate with God in his mission and those who do not is not identical with the line between those who attend church and those who do not. It is not even identical with the line drawn between those who call themselves Christians and those who do not. John G. Gager has said:

It is in terms of the "outsider," the hearer of the Gospel, that the life and proclamation of the local Christian community is to be judged and conceived. The basic truth of this affirmation is that even the most solid of church members is himself an "outsider" and that every element of

123

church order is but a provisional and limited response to specific situations.[7]

Every Christian missionary who travels to another country and deals with a language and culture quite different from his own knows what it means to be an outsider, often in a very painful way. He is strange. He may dress differently from most people. He certainly cannot speak the language of the country to perfection. He may eat different foods and follow different customs. No matter how hard he may try to achieve identification with the culture to which he goes, he is likely to be an outsider for the rest of his life. This is part of being a foreign missionary. Moreover, there is a symbolism here that has significance for every Christian individual and congregation. A foreign missionary is not merely a symbol of the strangeness of another culture. His presence in a new land, motivated by his understanding of a Christian calling, is in reality a symbol as well of the strangeness of the gospel, a strangeness which applies to every one of us. The gospel of Christ does not quite fit any of us: we do not easily receive it or fully live by it. Its demands are strange, and its promises we do not comprehend.

As to the gospel we are all outsiders. It is bread we do not always care to eat; yet as one outsider to another we may participate in evangelism, as D. T. Niles' famous phrase has it, as "one beggar telling another beggar where to find bread."

### THE NEED FOR DISCIPLINE

Fourth, New Testament church forms indicate an appreciation for the need of order and discipline. Paul puts it succinctly, following upon a series of admonitions concerning the way Christian meetings should be held, by saying, "Let all be done decently and in order" (I Cor. 14:40). Beneath this counsel is something far

---

[7] John G. Gager, "The Local Christian Community in the New Testament, A Monthly Letter About Evangelism," No. 7, October 1963, published by the World Council of Churches, Division of World Mission and Evangelism, page 4.

more important than the mere maintenance of propriety and decency. The need for discipline is rooted in the message of Jesus and the demands of the gospel.

The radical nature of Jesus' teaching is particularly evident in the Sermon on the Mount. Not only harmful acts but anger itself is condemned. Concealed lust, as well as adulterous acts, is also condemned. Men are to love both friends and enemies, especially enemies. Man is called to full integrity and purity of heart. The sermon calls on man to turn the other cheek when he is attacked and to give to the man who requests a loan. What does a congregation do with this kind of demand? There have been a multitude of interpretations of these words, some urging that they merely present an ideal attitude, others saying they refer to a future kingdom into which we have not yet entered, still others indicating they have to do with an interim between Jesus' ministry and the soon expected end of this world. Whichever interpretation is accepted, the radical nature of the demands makes clear that those who undertake to follow Jesus are subject to a requirement that is both urgent and exacting. Carelessness either in personal or corporate life will not do to meet these demands. These words cannot be spiritualized away to some other realm, either in the present or the future.

Kee and Young remind us that it is impossible to avoid the conclusion that Jesus often meant exactly what he said! [8] At a very minimum we must believe that Jesus intended that his words be taken seriously; and if we do this, the conclusion is inescapable that Christians have to take upon themselves the responsibility, individually and collectively, of a disciplined life. This became necessary in the early days of the Christian church as opposition mounted and the costs of discipleship became greater. Some kind

---

[8] Howard C. Kee and Franklin W. Young, *Understanding the New Testament*, Prentice-Hall, Inc., Englewood Cliffs, N. J., 1957, page 137. Chapters 6 and 12 of this book are especially helpful in presenting the early organization of the Christian church.

of orderly discipline was required to maintain the distinctiveness of the Christian community, to preserve the radical nature of the claims of Christ upon human life and society, and to provide for cohesiveness in the face of outside attack.

Early Christian groups show a great spontaneity in matters of organization. The ministry of the church was a spontaneous response to the action of the Holy Spirit. There were apostles, prophets, and teachers. But soon a more formal organization appeared. We begin to hear of elders, deacons, and bishops. Paul addresses his letter to the Philippians to "God's people, incorporate in Christ Jesus, who live at Philippi, including their bishops and deacons" (Phil. 1:1). Some were given special authority as leaders and counselors (I Thess. 5:12). The First Epistle of Peter contains a section in which the elders of the community are addressed with suggestions as to how they should exercise their authority (I Peter 5:1-4).

In time the elders came to be accepted as successors to the apostles, and among them appeared those who were leaders of special importance, the bishops. The bishop must exercise his authority wisely and be an example to the community. Among other things it is interesting to note that he should be ". . . faithful to his one wife, . . . not be given to drink, or a brawler, . . . and no lover of money" (I Timothy 3:1-7). Responsibilities increased. The care of widows was highly important (I Tim. 5:3-16). Prisoners had to be attended (Hebrews 13:3). Money was raised for persons in disaster areas, following Paul's example of raising money for the Jerusalem church in time of need. Conflicts between Christians had to be adjudicated. An order and a discipline evolved to meet these demands.

Particularly important were the central rites of the church: baptism and communion. It was early recognized that the manner of conducting these rites could not be left to chance. The earliest description we have of Christian baptism appears in the *Didache*:

Concerning baptism, baptise thus: Having first rehearsed all these things, "baptise, in the name of the Father and of the Son and of the Holy Spirit," in running water; but if thou hast no running water, baptise in other water, and if thou canst not in cold, then in warm. But if thou hast neither, pour water three times on the head "in the name of the Father, Son and Holy Spirit." And before the baptism let the baptiser and him who is to be baptised fast, and any others who are able. And thou shalt bid him who is to be baptised to fast one or two days before.

Holy Communion, originally simply a part of a fellowship meal, increasingly got separated off into a liturgical observance. It should be conducted according to specified ways and in a particular manner. Kee and Young highlight a reason for this:

. . . one of the principal reasons for this development was the church's battle against the strange teachings that were being promulgated by false prophets. These teachings were as dangerous to the Eucharist as to any other aspect of Christian faith and practice, and in his letters Ignatius repeatedly insists that the Eucharist can be held only where bishops, presbyters, and deacons are present. Ignatius knew that in some churches members were partaking of the Eucharist isolated from the main body of Christians and under unauthorized ministers. Others were refusing to participate at all. He sensed a real danger here, for once the rite stopped being shared by all Christians, the unity of the community would be threatened.[9]

Other examples could be listed to show how early in the New Testament period congregational structures evolved with careful attention to discipline and order. Whether or not this should have happened is an irrelevant question. It did happen. Further, it almost certainly had to happen so that the Christian community could know itself and the demands upon it, and could at the same time reach out to the world around it with the power and attraction that can only come from a disciplined and orderly movement. To those who argue that the church must do away with all struc-

---

[9] Kee and Young, *op. cit.,* pages 380-381.

tures, the New Testament offers no comfort. Those who argue that we should get back to New Testament structures and use them alone the New Testament confronts with a variety of structures implying that structures are to meet the needs of mission and are not in and of themselves fixed for all time. To those who argue for freedom in devising new structures the New Testament offers great encouragement, provided this freedom is tempered by a discipline that takes the demands of Christian living seriously and by an order that provides a channel through which Christian power and witness may flow.

In our day one of the noteworthy developments in Christian circles is the amazing increase in a variety of movements which in one way or another protest against what is seen to be the failure of the church to insist on a discipline. The Church of the Saviour of Washington, D.C., mentioned earlier in this book, is a community that insists on a prolonged period of depth study prior to membership and insists on a sacrificial commitment in time, service, and money from every member. Much of the appeal of small fellowship or cell groups is that they provide a cutting edge of discipline for every participant, bringing to bear the power and support of the small group upon every member to persist in prayer, Biblical study, total life stewardship, and witnessing service. Much of the criticism of the persons most deeply committed to church renewal in our day is aimed at the apparent lack of concern for, or the insistence on, certain disciplines which Christians voluntarily take upon themselves to bring their total outreach into a distinctiveness and a power that only such a discipline can provide.

The Methodist board of missions has recently become aware again that in missionary recruitment the challenge offered by participation in a disciplined community draws a response from young men in our day that more traditional calls to missionary service have not evoked. In 1963 a call went out to recruit fifteen young men to be a part of what was called the Congo Team. The idea was that they would be carefully screened and selected, they would undergo special training, live together as a disciplined community in Belgium while studying French, and eventually go into the complexity and the upheaval that is the Congo, sustained by their discipline, to serve for a three-year period under the leadership and direction of the church there. The response to the call was immediate and impressive. The idea of a disciplined community was attractive rather than menacing. In June, 1964, the young men selected came together and began this new experience. At this writing, almost a year later, the team is completing its period of language study. It has been both a difficult and a fruitful year. The tensions and stresses of living and learning together have been very real and very great. The intensive discussion of motivations, purposes, and faith has not been at all an easy thing. Yet apparently, out of it all, there has developed both a discipline and an acceptance by the members of each other based on the acceptance they feel God offers them. This development has allowed new insights into the meaning of the Christian faith and an opportunity for a healing relationship in which group members could open up freely with even some of their most intimate concerns and know that the community would understand and help. The group is still in a period of preparation. The meaning and nature of their service in the Congo is still a thing of the future. It is probable that they will be separated and spread out in many different tasks in the Congo. Whatever lies ahead, it is likely that this initial period of disciplined group experience will make its mark, in the lives of the members of the team themselves as well as in the significance of their service to the church and to the Congo as a nation.

## SHAPED BY EXPECTATIONS

Fifth, *New Testament church forms are infused with an expectation of great hope.* We know that the Christian message proclaims a hope of great meaning for the present and the future, but we are

129

not so apt to realize that this hope, so central to the Christian gospel, must have its reflection in the forms and structures of the congregation itself. Hope appears to be more a part of the content of the message than a built-in part of the church structure. And so it is. But if hope is so central to the life of the church, it is proper to ask how this central element of our faith relates to the way the community shapes its life.

From its inception the early Christian community fixed its gaze upon the time when God would complete his transforming work. This mood of expectancy was very much a part of the Hebrew prophetic tradition which looked forward to the coming of the Messiah. The kingdom of God was at hand. The new age for which Judaism had longed was now beginning. What Jesus was doing proved that this was so. "But if it is by the finger of God that I drive out the devils, then be sure the kingdom of God has already come upon you" (Luke 11:20). The time of fulfillment was expected to come momentarily. Yet, though already present among men in one sense, the full coming of the kingdom was still in the future. The Son of Man would have to come again in glory and victory (Mark 8:38: Luke 11:24). The early church took this quite literally and expected a second coming of Jesus. The community lived between the time when the new age had dawned and the time when the kingdom would come in its completeness. It prayed, "Thy kingdom come," and it waited.

The expected consummation did not come as anticipated. As months dragged out to years, the community had to reassess its hope and reevaluate its expectation. A vivid opportunity for this reexamination came when, late in the first century, the Christian church faced the demand to participate in worship of the Roman emperor. The book of Revelation struggles with the nature of the church's response to this demand.

In cryptic language the author of Revelation attempts to offer insight into the problems of the Christian community of his day.

Since he saw the problem of emperor-worship as but one skirmish in the battle between God and the powers of evil, he concentrates on the ultimate hope Christians have as they work through a difficult crisis at hand. He foresees the coming of the Lion and the Lamb (Rev. 5:5, 6) who is Jesus Christ, coming in victory and humility, triumphant over God's enemies. There will be war (Rev. 6:2, the white horse), civil war (Rev. 6:3, 4 the red horse), famine (6:5, 6, the black horse), and plagues (Rev. 6:8, the pale horse). But in the middle of it all God is at work, and the community expects him to provide a final deliverance (Rev. 6:9-11). Bad as the present troubles were, the Christian community could hope for a peace and a victory that was sure. The final consummation is a "new heaven and a new earth" (Rev. 21:1) when the Lord God will reign forevermore (Rev. 22:5).

What did this hope mean for church structures? First, these forms are all *tentative and impermanent*. They exist only between the beginning of the new age and its fulfillment. There is nothing sacred in structure itself. The hope of eventual fulfillment renders them necessary only for a time. Today centuries have passed, but structures still are tentative, useful for a purpose but wholly secondary and modifiable.

Secondly, church structures which exist under the shadow of such a hope would have to be *consonant with the expectations* of the hope. Thus, for example, since God's acceptance and forgiveness were integral to the hope, the community should live and regulate its activity to prefigure and give evidence of that forgiveness in its personal relationships. The forms of worship and sacrament, service and administration, would have to embody concrete evidences of this forgiveness, which could be a present reality as well as an expected future gift.

Thirdly, church structures are to be *missionary;* for the hope is that God in his mission will break into the world with a new fullness that we do not yet know but which we do expect, and it is the church's task to prepare for this coming. Proclamation and witnessing service are highly urgent matters. In the light of this expectation it is inconceivable that the Christian community can sit back to enjoy its inner fellowship or close itself up to a select few, much less to a routine traditional observance of stale rituals unrelated to mission. Thus

... the church as it is pictured in the New Testament does not regard itself primarily as an organization, though it does organize in order to assign responsibilities. Nor is it a closed corporation, established to serve as the protector of the body of truth committed to it by God. Rather, the church is the community of those who are convinced that the God of history has acted decisively in Jesus Christ to achieve the redemption of his creation, to overcome the evil at work in it, and to bring the whole into subjection to his sovereignty. . . . Although the community's history has been one of conflict within and hostile pressure from without, it has refused to die in despair, but has continued through the centuries to live in hope.[10]

Many a congregation today must live by hope because little else remains. Persecution or severely restricted Christian activity force a new awareness of the essentials of faith.

The story came out of Communist China that in a banquet a Christian who dared not be overt in his faith took a piece of bread and unobtrusively but significantly broke it, and as he did, he said, "I remember." A few others round the table who noticed this quietly ate bread also. Moments later the same man took a glass of water and, prior to taking a sip, again said, "I remember." Others did likewise. That was all that was needed. The sacrament of Holy Communion had been reenacted, the Christian community was present, the hope was kept alive.

In one area of Cuba it became virtually impossible for children

---

[10] Kee and Young, op. cit., page 472.

to attend Sunday school because of government pressure. The teachers discarded the pattern of the past and organized themselves into small visiting teams who went around from home to home each Sunday to take the lessons to those who could not "go to church" to receive them. The hope of a future society without neighbor rivalries, internecine strife, and total submission to the state remains. Beyond that, channelled into the lives of Cuban children, this hope provides a destination and an anchor for Christians so easily adrift on stormy seas. For the hope just to be present is of itself meaningful as part of God's plan for history in that place.

The fact that most of us live in areas where as Christian communities we do not yet have our backs to so obvious a wall tends to minimize our emphasis on the Christian hope. We structure our community in terms of rapid membership gains, activities for the here and now, an identification of the kingdom with the present social order. Our perils are not so evident, but they are surely there.

There is a city of God which gathers up symbolically the hopes of the faith, and towards this city the congregation in mission moves. To understand the urgency of its expectation and the profundity of its present meaning makes all the difference, whether in New Testament times or in the hopeless yet hopeful world of the twentieth century.

* * *

## Questions for Discussion

1. List as many different types of congregational forms and structures as you can remember from the New Testament.
2. What does it mean to you that "the Word sets the agenda for the church"? Does this in any way conflict with the statement that "the world sets the agenda for the church"? Are these statements complementary?
3. How is your congregation oriented to the outsider? What specific changes would you welcome in your congregation to emphasize the

congregation's responsibility to the outsider? Are you an outsider, or an insider, or both?

4. Read through the Epistle to the Ephesians. What kind of congregational forms does the author of the Epistle have in mind as he writes?

5. What does it mean for church forms to be infused with hope? Can you point to what this might mean in your own congregation?

## chapter VI

## IMAGES FOR NEW CONGREGATIONS

*The search for new congregational forms is aided by the projection of new images that help envisage the goal towards which we may move. The dual-centered ellipse, the intruder, and the boundary-crosser are such images.*

The way in which we picture ourselves determines to a large extent the direction and outcome of our lives. We tend to become what we conceive ourselves to be. Though often unconsciously, images do make a difference in our lives. Dr. Paul S. Minear has indicated several functions of images in a book that deals with pictures the church has of itself.[1] Among these functions he states that an image may be simply a tool of expression designed to help men describe something already known. A boy may describe his father as an "old fossil" or as a "powerhouse." Such picture language tells its own story about the way in which the son sees his father.

Then again an image helps to perceive a reality that cannot be measured or seen objectively. Love cannot be measured, but we constantly use images to describe it: it is "sweet" or "earthy" or "out of this world." Another function of an image is to aid in self-understanding. I may see myself as a "solid rock" or as a "gay

---

[1] Paul Minear, *Images of the Church in the New Testament*, Westminster Press, Philadelphia, 1960.

playboy" or as a "cool, reasoning thinker!" These images may be very inaccurate, or they may be quite descriptive of the truth; but in either case they serve a function. We use images as tools of expression and understanding.

The New Testament is full of images to describe the church: it may be a rock, or a bride, or salt, or mother, or seed. The response men make to the very existence of the church depends largely upon what their picture of the church is. If they see it solely as a pile of rock on the corner of Main and Market streets, they react one way to it. If they conceive of it as a bastion of defense against some foreign ideology, they react another. Perhaps, to paraphrase Charles Caleb Colton, they will "wrangle for it, write for it, fight for it, die for it; anything but live for it." If they see the church as a defensive minority, their relationship to it is quite different from what it is if they picture it as a growing institution sweeping the world.

The point need not be labored. Images do make a difference. Our concern is inwardly to appropriate new images that might be helpful in our understanding of the role of the church in the kind of a world in which God carries on his mission today, images faithful to the New Testament, and images that might have some pulling power upon us as Christians to draw us towards greater faithfulness in congregational life. We shall attempt to do so under three major headings: (1) the shape of the local congregation, (2) the location of the congregation, and (3) the direction of movement of the congregation. At most the use of images can only be suggestive. To push an image too far is to distort it.

## The Shape of the Congregation

It may seem strange that throughout our study thus far we have not yet attempted to define what a Christian congregation is. We have assumed that each reader has some concept in his mind of what a Christian congregation is or is supposed to be. We have further assumed that an attempt at definition would be fruitless. A group of Methodist church leaders sat down in 1964 to try to write out a statement of "the marks of a congregation." The question before them was "What distinguishes a Christian congregation from any other grouping that is not a Christian congregation?" In short order no less than forty-five marks of a Christian congregation were listed. Some of these were repetitive and overlapping, but the attempt illustrated the wide range of connotations we associate with the word. The immense variety of groups which can be described as Christian congregations heightens the problem; yet the variety itself is perfectly in line with the New Testament background, which, as we have seen, provided for ample diversity in congregational structure.

The Central Committee of the World Council of Churches at its January, 1965, meeting in Enugu, Nigeria, received an interim report from the Department of Studies in Evangelism which wrestled with the problem of structures of missionary congregations. This report, in a footnote, states: "By 'congregation' we mean any form of Christian gathering." On the face of it, this would seem too broad a statement. At least it would be too much to say that each time Christians come together they form a congregation by the simple fact of being together. If Christians gather to play bridge or to attend a play or to eat lunch together, the group formed is not a Christian congregation. Such groups, however useful or valid in themselves, are not necessarily related to a mission. The one stress we have insisted upon throughout this study has been that a Christian congregation is tied to mission. The World Council report referred to above implicitly recognizes this and probably would not equate a "Christian gathering" with just *any* grouping of Christians. The same report states, "A truly missionary congregation is a community for others." This description ties the congregation to mission.

A simple picture of the shape of a congregation that may serve as an image is the ellipse. Geometrically an ellipse has two centers, two foci. Let one center symbolize for us the gathered nature of the congregational community and the other the scattered congregation. Both, together, are the congregation. Here is a simple diagram:

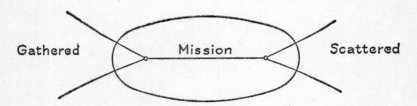

The gathered congregation has one major function, which is the preparation for mission. The scattered congregation has as its main function the participation in mission. Mission is at the very heart of the life of the congregation. All that happens in the gathered life of the congregation is determined by the nature of the mission. All that happens in the scattered life of the congregation is equally determined by the mission.

The components of the preparation for mission are worship and study. The expression of participation in mission is witnessing service. Where either worship and study or witnessing service are missing, it is difficult to conceive that a Christian congregation is present.

Recently a group was considering the civil rights movement in the United States. Two statements were made. The first was that many groups that today call themselves Christian congregations, both North and South, are not really Christian. They fail to become involved in the racial struggle in witnessing service as an outgrowth of their worship and study.

The contention was that no matter what their worship and study might be, if it did not issue in participation with God in what seems to be a major issue for Christians in our country today, their gathering could not claim to be Christian. This is simply another way of saying that a gathering that provides solace, comfort, and pleasant fellowship for those who gather is insufficient to create a Christian congregation. Whatever legitimate differences might exist within the group about proper ways to face the racial problems of our day, a Christian congregation can hardly check out of the issue and maintain its right to consider itself a Christian congregation. To gather for worship and study that issues in no participation in mission is contradictory of the nature of a Christian congregation.

The second statement made at the civil rights meeting was that if a group of concerned Christians participates in a picket line for racial integration of, let us say, a New York City building union, this group by its very involvement in a mission thereby constitutes itself as a Christian congregation. I question this. However laudable the aim of the group, action in mission without some kind of worship and study related to it does not constitute a Christian congregation.

The symbolic life of worship, which nurtures a community's life and purposes, is not an additional frill or a Sunday exercise that may or may not be superimposed on the congregation's action program. It is an essential, integral, and necessary part of the life and shape of a Christian congregation. Worship, thus, is a part of the structure of a Christian congregation.

Worship and study without participation in mission are truncated. Action in mission without worship and study is much like a cut flower whose long-range prospects are very limited and whose Christian significance is severed from the source of continuing life.

Worship is the conscious response of the congregation to the God who created us all and who calls us to be his people within his mission. In public worship we join to act out dramatically something of the interior meaning of our relationship to him. We recognize before him our corporate responsibility, our dependence upon him, our need for renewed vitality and resources. Symbolically we give ourselves to him in the offering in order that he may use us fully in his mission. To the promises conveyed to us through the reading of the Scriptures and to the spoken desire of the soul in praise, thanksgiving, confession, intercession, and petition we say "Amen." We thereby affirm our individual place within the totality of the Christian congregation, with all the responsibility and burden this implies. In private, personal worship we enter into our own communion with God at levels we may not even dare to share with the community; yet even as we do, we are a part of the community in mission, never wholly alone, never separated from the Christian congregation as such.

Study is equally a part of this congregational gathered life. The nature of the study will vary immensely, but always in one sense or another it will be a reflection upon, and analysis of, the meaning of God's revelation in Christ and the nature and meaning of God's present activity in the world. The compass of this study may include the Scriptures, modern art, classical poetry, medieval music, the daily newspaper, and forecasts of the future. Its effort is to understand the nature of God and of his world as a preparation for more effective participation in his mission. It is not purely academic, nor is it carried on for its own sake. It is purposive and operational, destined to prepare the congregation for a more significant concrete response in the specific tasks taken up in God's mission.

Seen in this light, the congregation in worship and study is a training center, a preparing community, a staging area for the mission which is central to its life. The seriousness of this preparation has led many congregations to recognize the importance of writing down on paper, often quite succinctly, the specifics of their understanding of mission and of the purposes the congregation attempts to carry out. There is nothing quite like the difficult exercise of attempting to work out on paper a statement of the creed of the congregation, a formulation of long-range objectives, an analysis of the present state of the congregation, and a detailed step-by-step blueprint of ways in which the congregation will carry forth its mission in consonance with its creed and stated purposes. To some this exercise may seem too academic, but it has the virtue of forcing the participants in such a writing to engage in a real confrontation with the bases of faith and meaning of mission. As a tool it is most helpful.

On the other side of the ellipse, the scattered congregation is involved in witnessing service, a natural outgrowth of the worship and study of its gathered life. Here the congregation is best seen as a community of ministries. Men and women of widely varying skills and training engage in the ministries for which their talents and peculiar individual preparation fit them, leavened by the training of the gathered life of the congregation. Equipped for ministry, they now seek out their special point of mission and engage in it.

The congregation in the world is the laity at work. Here the congregation is present, not for its own sake nor for its institutional life, but for the sake of the world itself, a "community for others." Here the plans and schemes and motivations generated in worship and study get a workout. They may flounder, succeed, or fail in the complex task of doing something by way of concrete presence at the point of God's activity in a limited chunk of history.

Size, as a characteristic of such an "elliptical" congregation, is literally unimportant. It may be a nine thousand member Dallas church, an ecumenical team in East Harlem, an industrial mission in Tokyo, a "house church" in Brazil, or a tiny cell of searching Christians in Kentucky. The World Council report, referred to previously, speaks repeatedly of "little congregations" which have "arisen through earnest engagement with the growing number of new crises and needs of contemporary society." All have in common the two foci: a gatheredness for worship and study, and a scatteredness for witnessing service in mission. Central to all is mission.

Some examples may serve to illustrate emerging structures that in widely different ways sense the meaning of such an ellipse. A new congregation arose in West Islip, Long Island, in a nucleus of population that sprang from a 1963 movement of eighty-one families. These families concentrated on Bible classes in homes. They agreed to offer their service to other families of the community desirous of studying the Bible. They made a census of the area to see who might be interested. Three hundred and four families invited the lay teachers to come in, while 462 others enrolled in a Bible correspondence course. The central purpose of the congregation was to help make the Scriptures known and understood by non-church folk of the community. To do so, it had to train its own members to know and teach the Scriptures. It had to make detailed plans of strategy as to how it would approach and serve in mission in the community. A month-by-month strategy for the year ahead, with clear goals, was written down on paper. With a membership of 279 the 1965 aim was one hundred neighborhood classes per week in session throughout the year. In 1964 membership had grown from 148 to 279; Sunday morning worship attendance had started at 225 and grown to 364; and Sunday morning Bible classes had started at 215 and grown to 341. Such figures are not too important as compared to the central concern of the congregation to prepare itself for the specific mission it has undertaken: presenting the study of the Scriptures to non-Christians on Long Island.

A totally different sort of project has developed in Port Harcourt, Nigeria. Port Harcourt is a boom town of about a quarter million population, sprawling for fourteen miles in disorderly growth. The Diobu slum brings together over ninety thousand inhabitants jammed together in filth and desperation, scarcely a mile away from luxurious dwellings of the well-to-do. The parish churches were overwhelmed with the problem. Some kind of united approach was necessary if any impact could be made. The first step was study.

The Port Harcourt Christian Council had a survey made, evaluated the need, and set out on a broad-based approach to the entire Port Harcourt area. Two team ministries were set up, one an Industrial Team to deal with the myriad problems dumped on the city by rapid industrialization and the other a Social Service Team to provide identification with and service to the Diobu slum.

Out of this initial effort, on a wholly interdenominational basis, the Port Harcourt Project has moved to provide an industrial chaplaincy to ship workers (every ship in port is visited monthly, which means from 100 to 120 visits per month), a Workers Discussion Group, a Trade Unions Discussion Group, classes for the workers, management-union seminars, an Industrial Library, a multi-racial school, a Trade School for Women, social service for slum dwellers, adult literacy classes, youth clubs, clean-up campaigns, plans for community centers, a Research Division, and so on and on.

This entire program brings together something more than what we generally think of as a single congregation, but in a real sense it is precisely that: a group of concerned Christians of many churches engaged in a mission in which they find God intimately involved and for which they prepare themselves with worship and study to deal effectively with a wide area of evident human need.

Whether in a tiny cell group, in a traditionally structured residential congregation or in a wide-ranging ecumenical project, the Christian congregation is helped by this elliptical image, with mission as central, with preparation for mission in worship and study as its gathered focus, and participation in mission in the community and the world as its scattered focus.

143

## THE LOCATION OF THE CONGREGATION

A second, and quite different, image that may assist us in understanding the missionary nature of a congregation is that of the intruder. An intruder is one who enters unexpectedly, and without invitation, into a locality where he is neither wanted nor awaited. This is hardly the picture of the church we normally have, but its strangeness is a reason for suggesting it.

The whole study of the missionary structure of the congregation runs up against the problem of the proper locale of the congregation. If we can have some idea of the shape of a congregation, suggested by the ellipse, it is more difficult to determine the place at which that congregation should exist.

The problem is that most of us have long since decided that there is a proper place for a congregation, which is generally associated with a residential area. No one would dispute the fact that this is a proper place for a congregation, given the high importance of residential areas to everyone who lives in them, but the difficulty emerges when that area is seen as the most important or sole locality for the life of the congregation.

To confine the congregation to a section of the community where people gather to sleep and constitute a family unit is to confine it too much. Hence the suggestion that, to break out of this pattern, we think of the church as an intruder in the very places where it is least wanted and where, by and large, no one save God wants it. There is reason to believe that this image is not altogether far-fetched. In the Old Testament the spokesmen for God are usually very much the intruders. The prophets intruded into the life of Israel and the councils of the mighty with denunciations and prophecies that were not desired in the least by anyone.

The incarnation of our Lord Jesus Christ was a majestic intrusion into the history of the world, a world that was looking for a messiah but hardly expected the strange Messiah it received.

The early Christian communities were thorns in the flesh of the Roman Empire, as they went about turning the world upside down.

The missionary movement of the church, from its earliest days to the present, has meant intrusion after intrusion by men and women who have felt themselves constrained by God to move into areas of the life of the world where they were not asked and where the majority of the residents would gladly have seen them depart at the earliest possible moment. I believe it was D. T. Niles who stated that "today missionaries are needed and asked for, but not wanted." It is one of the strange features of the life of a foreign missionary that today he goes to a country where in most instances the church present there has asked him to come because his skills are required, yet he gets there only to find out that he is an intruder, one who for any number of reasons in not really wanted even by some of those who most insistently asked for him to come.

In protest against the idea that the proper location for the Christian congregation is the place where it is at home, wanted, and comfortable, the image of the intruder is useful. It suggests that a Christian congregation must forever wonder where it should be present where it is not at all at home, where it is unwanted and uncomfortable. To be sure, the criterion for the proper sphere of action of a congregation is not solely the fact that it is unwanted.

The criterion for the proper sphere of action of a congregation is the activity of God at a particular place in the world. The congregation goes there as part of its mission to participate in his mission. The remarkable experience that ensues when a congregation enters that sphere is that so often it is clearly an intruder in this area of life, an area in which it must continue to intrude in order to be a participant in God's mission.

In early 1964 an Australian Methodist minister was appointed to a part of Sydney called Kings Cross, in the most densely populated square mile in the southern hemisphere. This square mile is the center of Australian entertainment. There was no church to speak of working in that area. Prostitution, homosexuality, drug addiction, and sensation-seeking are all part of the Kings Cross landscape. The new minister was to contact, and work with, the "beatnik" community. Here surely the church would be an intruder! In an apartment he set up The Wayside Chapel of the Cross. He struck up friendships with the beatniks. An Upper Room Coffee Shop was organized. A Poetry Corner was set up, and the best poems and prose are published in a magazine called *Cross Beat*. Counselling is a daily part of the ministry to this group. The church is used for art exhibits, folk-singing, and above all for a serious search for truth in the midst of "redemptive involvement" in a very unlikely area for a Christian congregation—unlikely, that is, unless it sees itself as a necessary intruder into every area of life.

Teen-agers in low-income housing are not particularly eager to have Christian "do-gooders" intrude into their life in Huntsville, Alabama, or anywhere else. Somehow the Huntsville District Woman's Society of Christian Service decided to intrude on the Butler Housing project. A committee was formed with a sociologist, a nurse, a medical technician, a teacher, a minister, housewives, and others. A youth program began with a junior high party—as conventional as that! Youngsters in the backwash of the community began to get interested. A girl married at the age of thirteen found out that there were Christians who really cared about her. A group of young mothers was organized to discuss the problems they faced: alcoholic husbands, mentally retarded children, illness, poverty. A nursery for preschool children developed. A self-improvement study club served the needs of girls who knew little or nothing about personal care. Training in food preparation, crafts, and marketing was given. Other activities followed. It may be only a beginning. The point is that a Christian congregation deliberately went into an area where it was very much of an intruder in order to be part of God's mission there.

146

A city dump is a most unlikely place for a congregation to choose as a mission field. A Tennessee church did just that. Persons who lived off the garbage gleaned from the dump had been offered bus transportation to existing churches with no response. A youth group decided its mission would be to the dump, rather than in the development of a campsite for itself. A discarded store room was rented for $10 a month. They put a bell on top of the building and rang for the children to come. Two Negro children were among the first to come, and thus was born one of the first integrated Sunday schools in the South. Worship services and study sessions followed. Social service and nursing aid followed. School lunches were provided the first year for thirty-two children. School dropouts were reduced. Young people contributed what they could toward a building. A wealthy citizen heard of it and said, "Proceed with construction, and send me the bill for the amount needed to complete the building." The old truck-dumping garbage system gave way to a modern furrow disposal system in which the city takes pride. Aside from the value of the service rendered to many lives, the point we lift up here is that this youth group dared to intrude among those who had accepted their lot as scraps from a city dump.

J. Archie Hargraves in his provocative booklet, *Stop Pussyfooting Through a Revolution—Some Churches That Did*,[2] disputes the suggestion that, like Rip Van Winkle, the church is sleeping through the urban revolution of our day. He claims that, rather than sleeping through it, we as a church are pussyfooting through it. We slip through, neither understanding the major issues of the day nor coming to terms with our responsibility in the face of these issues. The thesis he advances is that "the clue to the church's effectiveness is the content and degree of its involvement with God in proclaiming and witnessing to his kingdom's coming and to *his*

---

[2] J. Archie Hargraves, *Stop Pussyfooting Through a Revolution—Some Churches That Did*, United Church Board of Homeland Ministries, New York.

involvement with the complex stuff that is his world." [3] A congregation seen as an intruder in such "complex stuff" serves two functions among others: it is a source of exposure, and it serves as a catalyst.

As a source of exposure, the intruding congregation ventures into areas not usually thought to be, in traditional terms, the concern of the congregation. Thus it places itself in a place where it may know, from near exposure, what is going on in the world around it. This is one of the secondary but important functions of foreign missions. It helps us as a church to be exposed to the reality of what is going on around us and to interpret back to the church at home something of the true nature of the world in which we live and to which we so easily become blind.

In the spring of 1965 the United States became embroiled in a Dominican Republic conflict. Our President sent American troops to the island. The issues involved were many. At this writing it is too early to know what the outcome of this venture may be. However, the presence of North American missionaries across Latin America has exposed the church in the United States to something of the continental reaction to this military step which otherwise we might not have sensed with such immediacy. We become aware of the reaction, which approximates sheer horror, concerning the meaning of this step for our future inter-American relations and the fear that in the not-too-long run this may have serious repercussions across the continent for our missionary intruding thrust. This is another way to say that an intruder has a heightened sensitivity to those among whom he lives, and thereby may convey to others something of the deeper significance of events that to the average observer seems less meaningful.

The other function of intrusion is to serve as a catalyst. An intruder is seldom ignored. His very "out-of-placeness" makes him stick out like a sore thumb. This enables him, if he acts wisely, to serve

---

[3] *Ibid.*, page 2.

as an agent for change. The Christian church worldwide is today a minority group. As population growth rates increase, the inevitable result is that the Christian minority is daily becoming a proportionately smaller minority of the total population. What is the role of a minority? This is a question missionaries in nations that do not have a Christian group must confront. Vast needs can be presented to the church, but in sober fact the church cannot begin to meet every human need, render every valuable service, undertake every load, much as it might like to. Ultimately the church—and this means each congregation—must choose its limited sphere of action. There it can discern God at work and then must endeavor to determine how its necessarily limited contribution can serve to set in motion a series of changes towards the end desired. In a word, it has a catalytic role to stimulate far greater changes for good than it can, of and by itself, bring about.

A major problem of church bodies as they engage in overseas missionary activity may illustrate this. What is the role of the church in community development projects around the world? Governmental and other funds are being poured into programs of community uplift. The church is challenged to seek funds to do likewise. There is no question that funds thus spent serve a useful purpose. The question a church has to ask, however, is whether there may be other purposes served by the same funds which might catalytically, though often less visibly, stimulate community improvement along with evangelistic growth. Should a half million dollars be invested in one ten-mile area to improve that community, or should it be invested in Christian training of rural extension workers to spread out over a much wider area to help stimulate agricultural improvement and responsiveness to the gospel on a wide scale?

The problem is how the church multiplies its relatively small resources to get the most far-reaching service out of its personnel and funds. No easy answers are forthcoming. Choices here are unclear, as anyone who has had to struggle with these problems knows well. But choices are necessary, and a helpful criterion is to seek out the most productive catalytic role for the church. This is not necessarily the path that will show up best in church statistics or institutional development.

For the local congregation much the same is true. If a congregation plans to embark on some particular service to the inner city, what are its purposes? For what reason does it intrude into that usually abandoned area of modern life? To help a limited number of persons living in proximity to the new store-front church? Yes, surely that, but beyond that, what else? The challenge to the inner-city congregation is to intrude into the life of the city with imagination and faith. It is a challenge to initiate pilot projects that may have a stimulative effect upon persons who otherwise might not be sparked into Christian change and service. It is a challenge to make agencies beyond the church aware of new possibilities because the church has broken new ground for them.

More often than not the fundamental concern of a congregation interested in catalytic change is the discovery and the Christian training of persons who can be scattered out through a given community to initiate pockets of change and new life and in turn stimulate others to do the same. For this reason more and more congregations are coming to the conclusion that their fundamental catalytic role is leadership development—the training of the laity, not for the purpose of serving the institutional church, but to spread out in the nooks and crannies of society to set in motion others who will see the possibilities of self-help and radically changed lives.

## The Movement of the Congregation

A third image, concerned especially with the dynamic movement of a congregation, is that of a boundary-crosser. In terms of the history of the Christian church this is not at all a new image. From

its earliest days the church has pushed out across almost every con-
ceivable boundary. The very word "missionary" conjures up a
sense of movement across some kind of boundary, whether geographical or social or otherwise. The reason for reasserting the centrality of this image is that in our twentieth-century world, characterized as it is by such rapidity and magnitude of change, the
temptation of the congregation is (1) to assume too easily that
most boundaries open to us have been crossed already, or (2) to
concentrate on the most proximate missions which are seen close to
home, including the reconversion of church members themselves,
so that boundaries out beyond the local congregation are blurred
out of sight, or (3) to recoil into a tight institutionalism which is
manageable and does not pose the uneasy threats to which any
boundary-crossing subjects a congregation.

The reason for trying to recover for our day the image of the
boundary-crosser is that the rapid developments in our world are
creating more boundaries than ever existed before. The walls of
separation that divide us often seem to grow higher rather than
the opposite. The wealthy nations increase their wealth and the
poorer nations move towards famine.

The specialization required to occupy positions of responsibility
in today's industry make us strangers to our neighbors who special-
ize in anything different from our own field. A biologist can hardly
talk to a miner who in turn cannot understand a theologian who
can scarcely pretend to know what an accountant is thinking!

Even as we are told that this is one world, we know that it is
two, East and West, and that each of these blocs is rent with boundaries that separate man from man, nation from nation.

This is an ecumenical age, but the fragmentation of church life
is so conspicuous that in Latin America alone it is estimated that
at least three hundred separate denominations are hard at work
seeking proselytes for their own understanding of the faith.

151

In an age of speedy travel much of the world makes it increasingly difficult to get visas to move smoothly over national boundaries for anything but the most transitory tourism. The boundaries of nation, of class, of knowledge, and of understanding are very much with us.

We believe that God in his action in history calls the church to be a reconciling and unifying agent, to take boundaries with utmost seriousness, and to cross and bridge them wherever possible.

The boundary-crossing may begin at home in the simplest way. Metz Rollins, Jr., of the United Presbyterian Church in the U.S.A., is quoted as saying:

The women's group or circle or sisterhood might get a new vision if a couple of meetings were adjuorned to the local night court. Family night suppers might take on a new dimension, and a breakthrough of middle-class smugness if the occasion became an encounter with leaders of the present revolution, the agitators. . . . There are those in our local congregation waiting for such a challenge. They are bored to tears with much of the activity . . . .

Crossing boundaries may mean bringing representatives of widely differing point of view into confrontation within the life of the congregation so that the tension of creative controversy may replace the lull of quiet meaninglessness. It may even mean a redrawing of boundaries the church has set for itself in order to break through long-established patterns that are questionable in our age.

Recently Methodist churches in the city of Montevideo, Uruguay, launched out upon an experimental exercise in boundary-crossing within their own organization. On the premise that the city of Montevideo should be seen as a unity and that the church in that city should think of itself as a unity, the traditional separation of the various Methodist churches there was challenged by a new system of organization and appointments.

152

For administrative purposes all churches were grouped into two major parishes, each with a team ministry of clergy and laymen. No one pastor is exclusively assigned to any one church. Questions pour in: Who is now my pastor? Whom do I call when someone in the family dies? To whom does a congregation's car belong? How can I know who will preach next Sunday? Preachers are rotated from pulpit to pulpit, each preaching the same sermon at every place (to discourage hearers who would follow the best speaker around!)

A common choir made up of representatives of each preaching center has been formed. Emphasis is given to adult education of potential leaders. Instead of traditional church commissions, as Emilio Castro puts it, "we are trying to create communities to minister in the critical sectors of the town: the big traffic networks, the groups of laborers occasionally on strike, the groups fighting for the welfare of the public school, and the like." This plan may work or it may be a magnificent failure, but no one doubts that the church is crossing boundaries that have long needed to be crossed, and in this there is true health.

The boundary the church has usually not known how to cross is the boundary of indifference. We have assumed in this study that a clue to that crossing is relevance to need, but D. Munby reminds us, "It is clear today that there is no easy transition from the fundamentally true to the immediately relevant." How to break through the wall of callous indifference to what God is doing in history is a major concern of the church, quite aside from any concern for preserving its life or institutionalism.

What boundary is it that separates the fundamentally true from the immediately relevant? A report came out of Britain which is both inspiring and discouraging. Entitled "A Mission's Failure—The Story of One Church in Pagan Britain," by the Reverend Nicolas Stacey, it describes the unvarnished facts of a tremendous effort of nearly five years to make a real impact in a section of Woolwich. Everything was tried. There was concentration on lay leadership. Skilled clergy of the finest training were used. Visitation was massive ("In our parish those who get on get out" into the community). Publicity was formidable. The church building became a seven-day-a-week beehive of activity from 7 A.M. to 10 P.M. The group ministry spent two hours daily in prayer. Community needs of a vast variety were met. A ministry to those contemplating suicide was provided.

Plenty of boundaries were crossed. But what was the net result? Too pessimistically, I believe, Stacey reports: "We have quite obviously failed." He reports on a new experiment, born out of what he considers a five-year failure:

We hope to appoint a paid lay bursar to run the parish, and most of the clergy of our staff will take secular jobs, leaving their evenings free for spiritual counselling, leading lay training-groups, sick-visiting and so on . . . secular [structures] determine the shape and tone of the world. If the Christian has anything to say, he must say it from within them.[4]

And so another attempt, a new form, is sought out for experiment. Another effort is made to break the barrier between the religious and the secular. Another try at relevance in keeping with God's mission gets under way.

Such a note may seem to be too uncertain, too open-ended, too ambiguous, for the conclusion of a study of the search for new congregational forms. But it portrays the restless agony of the search. To accept the dreary state of smug satisfaction with occasional visible gains is the ultimate defeat. And simultaneously to close the mind to every vibrant new search for a boundary to cross turns the congregation itself into a boundary which God must

---

[4]Nicholas Stacey, "A Mission's Failure—The Story of one Church in Pagan Britain, A Monthly Letter About Evangelism," No. 6, June 1965, published by the World Council of Churches Division of World Mission and Evangelism.

either skirt or destroy. Where the agony of search is swallowed into the deadliness of indifference, hope for the congregation flickers faintly. It is precisely the agony of search that spells out the hope. Privileged to have received knowledge of God's truth and to recognize the impact of his redemptive work among us, we give thanks that he has claimed us, even us, by his Word in his world for no other purpose than to be a part of his mission.

\* \* \*

## Questions for Discussion

1. What are the major tasks for a "gathered" congregation? What are its major tasks when it "scatters"?
2. How is your local congregation structured to be a training community?
3. Are residential congregations outmoded? If in some sense they are, what new congregational forms should replace them?
4. Do you find the concept of a congregation as an "intruder" helpful? Why or why not?
5. If a congregation should cross boundaries, what are the five most significant boundaries you feel your congregation should try to cross within the next year?

# for further reading

## ON THE MISSIONARY STRUCTURE OF THE CONGREGATION:

WILLIAMS, COLIN, *Where in the World?* New York: National Council of the Churches of Christ in the U.S.A., 1963.

WILLIAMS, COLIN, *What in the World?* New York: National Council of the Churches of Christ in the U.S.A., 1964.

WINTER, GIBSON, *The Suburban Captivity of the Churches.* New York: Doubleday, 1961.

## ON CHRISTIANITY AND HISTORY:

VAN LEEUWEN, AREND TH., *Christianity in World History.* Edinburgh: Edinburgh House Press, 1964.

## ON THE BIBLICAL BASIS OF MISSIONARY OUTREACH:

BLAAUW, JOHANNES, *The Missionary Nature of the Church.* New York: McGraw-Hill Book Company, Inc., 1962.

## ON SECULARIZATION:

COX, HARVEY, *The Secular City.* New York: The Macmillan Company, 1965.

WILMORE, GAYRAUD S., *The Secular Relevance of the Church.* Philadelphia: The Westminster Press, 1962.

## ON THE MISSION OF THE CONGREGATION:

JONES, TRACEY K., JR., *Our Mission Today.* New York: World Outlook Press, 1963.

NILES, D. T., *Upon the Earth.* New York: McGraw-Hill Book Company, Inc., 1962.

WEBSTER, DOUGLAS, *Local Church and World Mission.* New York: The Seabury Press, 1964.

WARREN, MAX, *Perspective in Mission.* New York: The Seabury Press, 1964.

# index